HEROES OF HISTORY

Dwight Eisenhower

Supreme Commander

HEROES OF HISTORY

Dwight Eisenhower

Supreme Commander

JANET & GEOFF BENGE

Emerald Books
P.O. BOX 635, LYNNWOOD, WA 98046

Emerald Books are distributed through YWAM Publishing. For a full list of titles, including other great biographies, visit our website at www.emeraldbooks.com.

Dwight Eisenhower: Supreme Commander

Published by Emerald Books
P.O. Box 635
Lynnwood, WA 98046

Cataloging-in-Publication Data is on file at the Library of Congress.

ISBN 978-1-62486-142-0 (print)
ISBN 978-1-62486-143-7 (e-book)

First printing 2021

Printed in the United States of America

HEROES OF HISTORY

Abraham Lincoln
Alan Shepard
Ben Carson
Benjamin Franklin
Benjamin Rush
Billy Graham
Captain John Smith
Christopher Columbus
Clara Barton
Davy Crockett
Daniel Boone
Douglas MacArthur
Dwight Eisenhower
Elizabeth Fry
Ernest Shackleton
George Washington
George Washington Carver
Harriet Tubman
John Adams
Laura Ingalls Wilder
Louis Zamperini
Meriwether Lewis
Milton Hershey
Orville Wright
Ronald Reagan
Theodore Roosevelt
Thomas Edison
William Bradford
William Penn
William Wilberforce

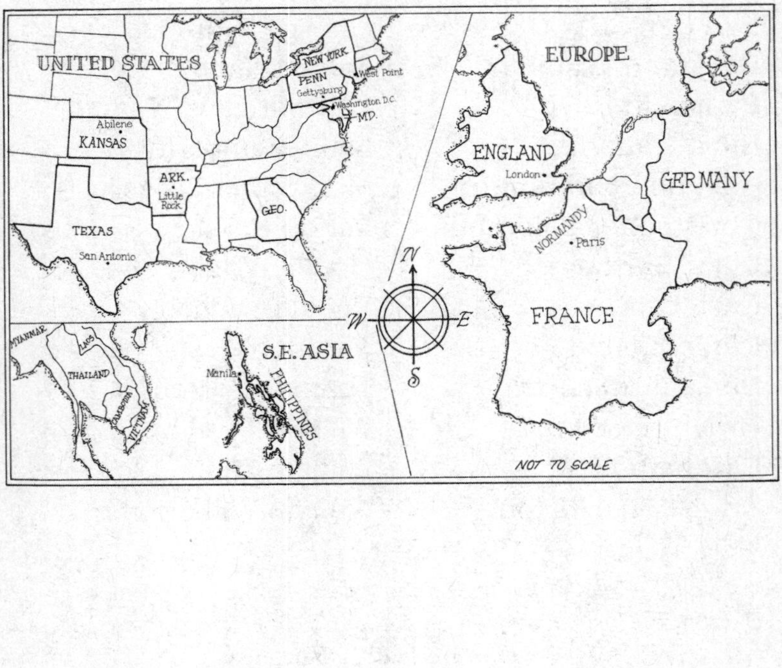

UNITED STATES
NEW YORK
PENN
Gettysburg
West Point
Washington D.C.
MD.
Abilene
KANSAS
ARK.
Little Rock
GEO.
TEXAS
San Antonio
EUROPE
ENGLAND
London
GERMANY
NORMANDY
Paris
FRANCE
N
W
E
S
S.E. ASIA
MYANMAR
LAOS
THAILAND
CAMBODIA
VIETNAM
Manila
PHILIPPINES
NOT TO SCALE

Contents

Chapter 1

A Momentous Decision

A huge storm—the fiercest June storm in over fifty years—is brewing north of us. Its full fury will be unleashed on the English and French coastlines by tomorrow morning," Captain James Stagg announced in his Scottish brogue, a grim look spread across his face.

Dwight Eisenhower looked out the window at the still, moonlit predawn. It didn't seem possible that the weather would deteriorate so completely in twenty-four hours. Yet Captain Stagg was a skilled meteorologist, and as difficult as it was, Dwight knew he had to order a twenty-four-hour postponement to the invasion.

Before dawn the following morning, howling winds and torrential rains buffeted the area. Dwight was relieved he'd ordered the postponement. A short time later, as Dwight awaited Captain Stagg's next weather update, the wind relentlessly rattled the windows of the building they were in.

Despite the foul weather, Dwight thought he detected a slight smile on the captain's face as he stood to speak. "Gentlemen," Captain Stagg began, "there will be a high front passing over England later today. It will push the storm farther south. This is good news. I calculate there will be a twenty-four- to thirty-six-hour window of good weather starting early tomorrow morning."

Following the weather update, Dwight listened to the rain pelt down outside. How much did he really trust the Scottish captain? The lives of millions of soldiers under his command rested on the answer. Eventually he stood and said simply, "Okay, we'll go."

Suddenly the room was alive with activity and noise. A myriad of things needed to be activated. There was no going back now. In twenty hours the first air bombing of the French coast would begin, followed several hours later by the first wave of troops attempting to land on the beaches. In the midst of all the noise and activity, Dwight took a moment to reflect. A lot—perhaps even which side would eventually win the war—rode on the decision he'd just made. As a boy growing up in Kansas, he could never have imagined he would be the one to make such a momentous decision that would affect the lives of millions of people around the world.

Chapter 2

A New Home

Seven-year-old Dwight Eisenhower lay in bed next to his older brother, Edgar. The sound of their parents' voices drifted into the boys' upstairs bedroom from below.

"It's an opportunity we can't turn down, David," Dwight heard his mother say. "This house is bursting at the seams, which is hard enough, but the real problem is keeping the boys corralled. There's no yard here, so they take to the streets. One minute Edgar's picking a fight with the MacDonald boy, and the next Dwight's jumped off a railing at the cattle yard and ripped his pants. The boys need a backyard where I can keep an eye on them and they have plenty of chores to stay occupied."

Dwight heard his father grunt. "We're better off renting this place. At least we can't get in over our heads financially."

"But think of it, David," Dwight's mother pressed. "If we had the land, we could grow enough food for all of us to eat. We could can fruit, pickle vegetables, and smoke fish and meat. We could have chickens and pigs. Abe's barn is big enough for dairy cows—we'll have our own milk and cheese." She paused a moment and then continued. "Besides, there's the trees Abe's planted—apples, cherries, pears. Think of it. The boys can eat their fill all summer long."

"It sounds like a lot of work. If I'd wanted to be a farmer, I would have been one years ago, Ida."

"The boys and I will do it," Dwight's mother said. "You work hard enough for us. Let me help. I'll supervise the boys. Before you know it, we'll have the food we need growing in our own backyard. All we'd have to buy would be kerosene and materials to make clothes. Besides, we could rent out the barn if we had to. Abe says it holds eight tons of straw. We could make it. I know we could."

After this there was silence, and all Dwight could hear was the click of his mother's knitting needles. He imagined his father had retreated into reading a book.

More than anything, Dwight hoped his mother would win the argument and his parents would buy Uncle Abe and Aunt Anna's house. Dwight knew the place well. His uncle and aunt had owned it since long before he was born. It consisted of three acres of land on which sat a two-story clapboard house and one of the biggest barns in the town of Abilene, Kansas.

Up until now, Uncle Abe, Dwight's father David Eisenhower's younger brother, had been a veterinarian and used his land to raise chickens, horses, pigs, and rabbits while Aunt Anna tended a chicken coop, a meat smoker, and a modest garden. At one end of the barn sat a gigantic table with an overhead hoist that Uncle Abe used when he did surgery on horses and cows. Dwight thought about the barn's high rafters to which the hoist was attached and wondered if he had the courage to climb them. He made up his mind he would try in the near future with his brothers. Dwight had four brothers, though he knew his oldest brother, eleven-year-old Arthur, probably wouldn't want to join in. Edgar and Dwight were the two daredevils of the family, always betting against each other that they couldn't do some death-defying feat. Arthur and Edgar were considered the "big boys," which often left Dwight playing with his five-year-old brother, Roy, or even having to look after the new baby, Earl. There was a big gap between Roy and Earl because when Dwight was four years old, another brother, Paul, had been born and had died of diphtheria a year later.

As he lay in bed that night, Dwight thought about Uncle Abe and Aunt Anna. They were members of a Mennonite group called the River Brethren Church. Sometimes Dwight's parents sent him and his brothers to Sunday school there, but Ida and David rarely went to the church themselves. Instead, his parents hosted a group from the International Bible Study at their house on Sunday afternoons. Uncle Abe, on the other hand, was an ordained River Brethren pastor, as was Uncle Ira, another of Dwight's uncles. And now Uncle Abe and Aunt Anna were selling everything they had and heading out to the open prairies in a "Gospel wagon." It reminded Dwight of the old-fashioned covered wagons that once carried pioneer families all the way to Oregon.

Dwight had heard Uncle Abe preach and thought he was good at it, and now he and Aunt Anna and two others were going to drive the Gospel wagon south and preach to homesteaders. Just five years earlier, in 1893, the Cherokee Outlet in Indian Territory, which neighbored Kansas to the south, was opened to white settlement. Many homesteaders had rushed to stake land claims in the area without the money to build a house or have any way of feeding themselves once they got there. Life on the frontier was lawless. There were no schools and no churches, and Aunt Anna told Dwight that she and Uncle Abe felt called by God to go to the highways and byways to proclaim the gospel. She called it a "highway and hedges" ministry.

A week after overhearing his parents' conversation, Dwight was delighted to learn that his mother had prevailed. The family would be buying and moving into the home that Uncle Abe and Aunt Anna were vacating.

Life soon became extra busy as Ida Eisenhower organized everything to be cleaned and packed for the move. The new house was located on Southeast Fourth Street, less than a quarter of a mile from the house they currently lived in. In fact, using a trolley they borrowed from the creamery where their father worked, Dwight and his brothers were able to push their mother's prized piano the short distance down South Second Street, then south on Buckeye Avenue to Southeast Fourth Street and their new house. Dwight couldn't have been happier.

Once the Eisenhower family was settled into the new place, chores began in earnest. The four oldest boys were assigned morning, afternoon, and evening tasks. Dwight's mother was fair in apportioning the chores. Once a week she prepared a roster on which each boy was assigned one set of tasks that rotated to one of the other boys the following week. Before long Dwight's life seemed an endless rotation of milking the two cows, weeding the corn, chopping wood, feeding the chickens, and collecting eggs. Since there were no girls in the family, there was no shirking on "women's work." All of the boys took turns cooking, washing, and mending clothes.

At first Dwight pouted when he had to do his chores, so much so that his mother told visitors to ignore her son's behavior. Eventually Dwight accepted chores as part of being in a large family and, unlike his brothers, began to like working around the house. He enjoyed peeling potatoes and chopping vegetables. He also liked standing beside his mother and helping her knead the twenty-seven loaves of bread she baked every week. And when fall arrived, he took pride in helping her put away cans of applesauce, cherry jam, and maple syrup. The only chore Dwight dreaded was washing Earl's dirty diapers outside on a washboard.

A month after the Eisenhower family moved into their new home on Southeast Fourth Street, just as Dwight was learning to read, he noticed a startling headline on the front page of the *Abilene Reflector*: "US Troops Land in Cuba!" Dwight's oldest brother, Arthur, explained to him that Cuba was an island southeast of the United States that was a Spanish colony. In February an American battleship, the USS *Maine*, lay at anchor in Havana Harbor, the island's largest port and capital. On the night of February 15, while still at anchor in Havana, the battleship exploded and sank, killing 260 crew members. Spain, Cuba's colonial overlord, was blamed for the calamity, and things rapidly went downhill from there. On April 21, 1898, the United States declared war on Spain, not just over that country's control of Cuba but also over Spanish control of other colonies, from nearby Puerto Rico in the Caribbean to Guam and the Philippines in the western Pacific Ocean. On June 22, US troops landed in Cuba.

Dwight was fascinated by all Arthur told him. He loved learning about wars, battles, and fighting, and he begged his oldest brother to read him the latest news about the fighting in Cuba. Theodore Roosevelt soon became one of Dwight's heroes of the war. He had been assistant secretary of the navy but resigned so he could lead a volunteer cavalry regiment known as the Rough Riders in Cuba. Dwight was enthralled with the stories he heard of the Rough Riders. The group was made up of miners, police officers, graduates from Harvard and other universities, cowboys, and Native Americans who rallied behind the leadership of Colonel Teddy Roosevelt. In early July, Dwight was delighted to hear how Roosevelt had led his Rough Riders in a charge to victory in the battle for the capture of San Juan Hill. Dwight and his brothers Edgar and Roy never tired of pretending to be Rough Riders, even though their mother frowned upon it. Members of both the River Brethren and the International Bible Study preached strongly against war and participating in such an activity.

Dwight loved to escape into his imagination, daydreaming of gun battles, warships, and overrunning barricades as he and his brothers laboriously planted corn, lettuce, potatoes, celery, peas, and pumpkins on their land. By now Earl was a toddler and had moved into the older boys' bedroom so the drawer in his parents' dresser could be readied to serve as the crib for another baby. Everyone hoped the sixth child would be a girl. It wasn't, and Milton Stover Eisenhower was born on September 19, 1899. Once more the Eisenhower boys resumed their diaper-washing and baby-minding duties.

During this time, Dwight and his brothers saw little of their father, who worked at the Belle Springs Creamery from seven in the morning until seven at night, six or sometimes seven days a week. When David got home, the family ate dinner together, after which David conducted a Bible reading and prayer. After that he buried his head in a book, reading for the rest of the night while Dwight's mother ushered the children through their nightly chores and then sent them off to bed.

Around the time Milton was born, Dwight made a new friend. Bob Davis was in his fifties—older than Dwight's father—but the two men were nothing alike. Dwight's father had a short temper, while Bob was a patient man. David Eisenhower loved to study his Pyramid of Giza map and read in *Zion's Watch Tower and Herald of Christ's Presence* magazine about how the world would soon end, while Bob couldn't read at all but was an excellent poker player.

Dwight met Bob at Davis Fishing Camp on the Smokey Hill River, and the two became instant friends. Ida Eisenhower gave Dwight permission to spend time with Bob as long as his chores and schoolwork were done. Soon Dwight was allowed to spend weekends at the fish camp, so long as he traded out his chores with one of his brothers. Dwight loved every minute he spent at camp, where Bob taught him how to set a fishnet, trap muskrats and mink, hunt ducks, and survive alone in the woods.

Bob was also a great storyteller. He'd come to Abilene, Kansas, as a young man in the 1860s and loved to tell stories about the place. Abilene was the first cow town, a place that sprang up from a few cabins at the end of the railroad line. In 1865, after the end of the Civil War, thousands of longhorned cattle were roaming the rangeland of Texas. This led to great herds of cattle being driven north from Texas along the Chisholm Trail, which crossed the Red River into Indian territory and then through Indian territory to Caldwell, Kansas. From there they kept heading north past Wichita and Newton until they reached Abilene. The cattle were then loaded into railcars and taken northeast to Chicago's Union Stock Yard, where the animals were butchered.

Eventually more railroad track was laid and the

railhead moved south to Caldwell. The great cow town days of Abilene had ended three years before Dwight was born. Dwight hated to think how he'd so narrowly missed out on seeing cowboys galloping into town, but at least he had Bob Davis to tell him stories about the town's past. Bob had known Tom "Bear River" Smith, a middle-weight boxer and ex-New York City policeman who agreed to take on the task of creating law and order in Abilene in 1869. Tom started by banning guns within the town limits and running several gunslingers out of town. He hunted down horse thieves and rounded up stolen cattle. Sadly, he lasted at the job only about a year, when he went to arrest two farmers charged with murdering their neighbor. Within minutes of arriving to make the arrest, Tom was shot in the chest by one of the men and died.

Bob told Dwight how the next man who volunteered for the job was Wild Bill Hickok, who also didn't last long. He left town in a hurry after accidentally killing his deputy in a shoot-out during a street brawl outside a gambling den.

As Bob spoke of these things, Dwight imagined the scene. The town hadn't changed much since those days. There were still boardwalks in front of the stores and stepping-stones at the street corners to help people cross the muddy streets. Horses were still hitched to posts outside the general store, but the saloons were gone. Although some of Bob's stories sounded far-fetched, Dwight knew that most of them were true and secretly wished his own family had stories to tell of Abilene's wild gunslinging days. But they had been living back East while all of this was occurring in Abilene.

In fact, Dwight thought the Eisenhower family history was rather boring. He knew the story well. His grandfather, the Reverend Jacob Eisenhower, was a preacher and leader in the River Brethren. The group's members all lived near each other in Elizabethville, a small enclave northwest of Harrisburg, Pennsylvania. Even though Jacob's ancestors had emigrated from Germany over 150 years before, Jacob and his children, including Dwight's father, still spoke German among each other. In 1878 a group from the River Brethren under his grandfather's leadership had decided to head west. They sold their farms, loaded everything they owned into boxcars, and purchased train tickets to Abilene. Dwight's father, who was fifteen at the time, along with two of his father's siblings, thirteen-year-old Abraham and nineteen-year-old Amanda, made the move with their parents. The rest of the Eisenhower siblings remained behind in Pennsylvania.

Dwight's mother, Ida Stover, was the only member of her family to live in Abilene. She was born and raised in Mt. Sydney, Virginia. At five years of age her mother died, and Ida was sent to live with her grandfather. When he died, she lived with her aunt and uncle, who didn't believe she needed an education past grade school. As a result, Dwight's mother struck out on her own and attended high school in Staunton, Virginia. To earn money to live on, she cleaned houses and baked pies. After graduating from high school and teaching grade school for two years, she ventured west in 1883 to stay with her brother, William, a Lutheran pastor in Lecompton, Kansas.

In Lecompton, Ida enrolled at the local Mennonite college, Lane University. A year later, Dwight's father began attending the college with aspirations of becoming an engineer. The two met, fell in love, and married, after which they decided to leave college and open a general store with the money Dwight's grandfather had given them as a wedding gift.

All of this had happened years before Dwight was born, and Dwight was much more interested in Bob Davis's tales of Wild Bill Hickok and Billy the Kid than he was in hearing stories about plowing the endless Kansas prairie to plant corn and wheat.

Dwight wanted to grow up and have adventures of his own. He thought about his father working in the creamery, and he knew one thing for sure—he didn't want to end up like that.

Chapter 3

How Was He Ever Going to Have Adventures?

Dwight grabbed a pillowcase and headed downstairs. It was the night of October 31, 1900—Halloween—and his heart beat with anticipation. The neighbors had decorated their porches with jack-o'-lanterns, cornstalks, and string cobwebs. But best of all, as far as Dwight was concerned, they had bags of candy crows and boxes of Cracker Jacks on hand to fill the pillowcases or bags of those who came calling at their doors.

Arthur and Edgar stood by the back door, pillowcases in hand, ready to find candy.

"Where do you think you're going?" Dwight heard his father say as he headed toward them.

"Trick-or-treating," Dwight replied.

His father shook his head. "I've already told you

you're not old enough. You are only ten. When you get older you can go, but not yet. And don't ask again."

Dwight grabbed his pillowcase and stomped out the door before his father could stop him. "I forbid you to go!" he heard his father yell as the door slammed behind him.

Outside Dwight stood at the corner of the house and weighed his options. He could disobey his father and run off down the street on his own. But he would eventually have to return home and receive the severe discipline his father would mete out. Or he could go back inside and spend Halloween with his little brothers and dream of what his older brothers were up to.

Truth was, Dwight didn't want to do either. He was too scared to disobey his father and too angry to go inside and be treated like a little kid. He stood at the edge of the Eisenhower property listening to the distant shouts of other children as they ran around in the dark collecting candy. It was too much for Dwight. He was stuck in the middle—too young to be allowed to do anything fun and too old to be content helping his mother with Roy, Earl, and baby Milton. How was he ever going to have adventures if he wasn't allowed out of the house?

Without thinking about it, Dwight walked over to a nearby apple tree and began pounding its trunk with his fists. His hands stung as he beat on the tree, but it didn't matter. His heart stung worse. He beat the trunk harder and harder until he could feel blood dripping from his clenched hands, but he didn't stop. Rage kept him going. On and on he pounded until he felt two hands grab his shoulders. "Stop it now!" he heard his father thunder.

Defeated, Dwight turned and walked into the house and upstairs without looking at anyone. He flopped down onto his bed, not caring that his hands were still bleeding. They throbbed with pain as he sobbed and tried to make sense of what he'd done. His mother opened the bedroom door and sat beside him on the bed. She held a can of salve and strips of cotton rag. Gently, one at a time, she took Dwight's hands and covered them in salve before bandaging them.

By the time his mother was finished, Dwight had stopped sobbing. "You know," she said quietly to him, "Proverbs 16:32 says, 'He that is slow to anger is better than the mighty; and he that ruleth his spirit than he that taketh a city.' You're going to have to ask God to help you tame your anger, Son. If you don't, you're going to lead a miserable life. A bad temper is going to hold you back from all of the good things you could do. It's important; the verse says it's more important to be in control of yourself than it is to conquer a city."

Dwight didn't respond. He heard his mother's words, but what could he say? He knew he had a terrible temper and that there were times, like tonight, when he lost it so badly he didn't know what he was doing. He knew he was hurting himself. The sting of the wounds on his hands would far outlast the disappointment of not being able to go trick-or-treating.

After that night, Dwight made an effort to control

himself and his temper, but it was difficult. Being able to spend time with Bob Davis helped a lot. Fishing, hunting, and listening to Bob's Wild West stories helped Dwight feel better about himself.

After the Halloween debacle, Dwight turned his attention to the 1900 US presidential election. This election was a rematch of the 1896 election where Republican William McKinley defeated his Democrat opponent William Jennings Bryan of Nebraska. In 1896, President McKinley's vice-presidential running mate had been Garret Hobart, but he had died in office. Now as he ran for reelection, President McKinley had chosen New York governor Theodore Roosevelt as his vice-presidential candidate. The choice excited Dwight: Teddy Roosevelt was still his hero from the Spanish-American War. On Election Day, November 1, 1900, when the votes were tallied, William McKinley and Theodore Roosevelt had handily beaten William Jennings Bryan. Dwight joined the Republican Party victory parade in Abilene and eagerly waited to see what new adventures Teddy Roosevelt might have as vice president of the United States.

Meanwhile, Dwight's last living grandparent, Jacob Eisenhower, was now seventy-four years old and tired of living alone. He wanted to move in with Dwight's family, but their 900-square-foot house was already bursting at the seams with two adults and six boys. To help alleviate the pressure for more space, Dwight's grandfather agreed to pay for a two-room extension to the eastern side of the Eisenhower house. By Christmas 1900 the addition was completed. Dwight's grandfather moved into one of the newly added bedrooms and his parents into the other. Arthur had always had his own tiny bedroom, so Edgar and Dwight moved into their parents' old room, while the smaller children stayed where they were. The extra space worked well for Dwight.

Grandfather Eisenhower also brought his horse and buggy with him. Sometimes when he was going out to visit River Brethren folk, he allowed Dwight to drive the buggy. Although he couldn't take the horse beyond a sedate trot, Dwight loved the freedom he felt rolling across the flat Kansas landscape filled with fields of wheat and corn.

On March 4, 1901, at an inauguration ceremony in Washington, DC, William McKinley was sworn in for his second term as president. Six months later, on September 6, American politics took a shocking turn. On that day President William McKinley visited the Pan-American Exposition being held in Buffalo, New York. While shaking hands with members of the public, the president was shot twice in the abdomen by an anarchist named Leon Czolgosz. The president was rushed to hospital for emergency surgery. It appeared at first that he would survive the assassination attempt, but his wounds became infected. Eight days later President McKinley died, plunging the nation into mourning. Following McKinley's death, Theodore Roosevelt was sworn in as the twenty-sixth president of the United States. Now Dwight had reason to pay even closer attention to social studies in school and see what the new president would do.

The following year, on October 14, 1902, Dwight

turned twelve. The school he'd been attending went only to fifth grade, so after his birthday he switched to Garfield School, which went to eighth grade. Dwight felt grown-up joining his brother Edgar, who was in eighth grade there.

Later in the year Edgar dropped out of Garfield School and took a job working for a local doctor. He didn't tell his parents what he'd done, and Dwight kept his brother's secret. The two brothers would start out together for school each morning, and then Edgar would diverge and head off to work. It took only a few days for news to get back to the Eisenhowers that their second son had quit school.

David Eisenhower severely disciplined Edgar for his deceptive behavior. Yet to Dwight's surprise, he allowed Edgar to continue working for the doctor rather than forcing him to return to school. Now Dwight was the only Eisenhower boy at Garfield School.

The most exciting event of Dwight's seventh-grade year was the first baseball World Series between the Boston Americans and the Pittsburgh Pirates that took place in October 1903. Honus Wagner of the Pittsburgh Pirates was Dwight's favorite player. Honus was not only a great shortstop but also a powerful batter. Unfortunately, he was bothered by an injury and didn't play well during the series. Dwight read the local newspaper report of each game. As much as he wanted the Pirates to win, they ended up losing to Boston by two games. The final game of the series was held on October 13, the day before Dwight's thirteenth birthday.

Toward the end of Dwight's seventh-grade year, Abilene united to remember one of their heroes—Tom "Bear River" Smith, about whom Bob Davis had told Dwight riveting stories. The town council decided that Smith's body should be exhumed and reburied in a prominent place in Abilene's cemetery on the north edge of town. On Memorial Day, Monday, May 30, 1904, Dwight joined a crowd to witness the unveiling of a loaf-shaped rock that stood over the new grave. A bronze plaque that was placed on top of the grave read like inspirational poetry to Dwight:

THOMAS J. SMITH
Marshall of Abilene, 1870,
Died, a Martyr to Duty, Nov. 2, 1870.
A Fearless Hero of Frontier Days
Who in Cowboy Chaos
Established the Supremacy of Law.

As summer approached, Dwight looked forward to earning money. His parents allowed each son to have a patch of garden in which to grow and sell whatever he wanted. Dwight put a lot of thought into this and decided on corn and cucumbers. It didn't take long for the Kansas sunshine to work its magic on Dwight's garden plot. Soon Dwight was harvesting ears of ripe corn and large cucumbers. He would then hitch up the wagon and head off to sell his crop to rich people living in mansions on the north side of the railroad tracks. Whenever he found himself on the northern outskirts of town, Dwight made a detour to visit Tom "Bear River" Smith's grave and pause for a moment to reread the inscription on the plaque.

The year 1904 marked the one hundredth anniversary of the departure of the Corps of Discovery under the leadership of Meriwether Lewis and William Clark, who had set out to cross and explore the western territory that the United States had gained from France in the Louisiana Purchase. To celebrate the anniversary, the Louisiana Purchase International Exposition was held in St. Louis, Missouri. At the same time, the 1904 Olympic Games were being held in St. Louis.

The 1904 Olympic Games, which officially opened July 4, were the third modern Olympics and the first to be held outside Europe. St. Louis was only 380 miles east of Abilene. Dwight's imagination ran wild as he read about the sporting events taking place there. In all, sixteen sports—including running, rowing, tennis, tug-of-war, golf, football, wrestling, and gymnastics—made up the Olympic Games. Dwight followed them all, keeping charts and tallies of who won what events. In gymnastics, a German American named George Eyser intrigued Dwight the most. George was competing with a wooden leg, since his left leg had been amputated following a train accident. Despite his wooden leg, he proved himself to be the world's best gymnast at the Olympics, earning six medals—three gold, two silver, and one bronze—in one day of competition.

Dwight used the money he earned selling summer corn and cucumbers to buy the latest *Wild West*

Weekly magazine, ice cream sodas, and a new pair of trousers for the upcoming school year.

At the end of summer 1905, Dwight enrolled in Abilene High School along with sixty-seven other students from eighth grade at Garfield School. The other half of his eighth-grade class went to work instead of entering high school. At first it seemed strange to Dwight to be the only Eisenhower boy in his school. His eldest brother Arthur should have been in twelfth grade, but he'd left home and found a job as a messenger boy for a bank in Kansas City. Meanwhile, his younger brother Roy was starting seventh grade at Garfield.

Dwight had no doubt he was entering the liveliest high school in the United States. This was because the classrooms consisted of converted offices in the town hall. Not only did the town hall house the high school, but it also accommodated the mayor's office, the fire station, and, most interestingly of all to Dwight, the jail.

On the first day of high school the fire marshal spoke to the boys in the class—all twenty of them—about their new responsibilities as volunteer firemen. He reminded them of the Great Fire in Baltimore, Maryland, that had raged earlier in the year. More than fifteen hundred buildings were destroyed, and thirty-five thousand people were left unemployed as a result. Although Abilene was a small town, the fire marshal reminded the boys that they might be called upon to play a vital role in saving the community from destruction. If they heard the bell in the building ring, the boys were to jump out of their seats and head downstairs to the fire station. The first boys there had to roll the fire truck out through the double doors onto North Broadway Street. By then the fire marshal would have learned where the fire was and would head the students and other City Hall employees in the right direction. Because the Abilene Fire Department didn't have horses, the volunteers had to haul the two-wheeled engine and water cart themselves. Dwight loved the excitement and challenge of working with a team to get a fire out as quickly as possible.

One morning, soon after starting at Abilene High School, Dwight arrived at school to find the corner of the building blown out. He soon learned that a prisoner in the jail cell on the ground floor had escaped after dynamiting through the cell wall.

Despite the distractions, Dwight settled into school. He enjoyed learning just about anything: English, geography, algebra, and his favorite subject—history. He found it easy to remember dates and facts, and he loved imagining ancient battles and conquering armies.

Halfway through his first year of high school, however, disaster struck. As Dwight ran along the boardwalk on Second Street, he tripped and fell. He was angry that he'd ripped the left knee out of his new store-bought pants but was grateful that his knee hadn't bled. All he saw were a few small red bumps on his kneecap. Dwight headed to school the next morning, but he noticed that his left knee felt hot and that the redness of the bumps spread as the day went on.

While sitting on the couch in the front room at home after school, Dwight began to feel woozy. The redness on his knee continued to grow bigger, and he could see a black line starting to branch out and climb up his thigh. The next thing Dwight remembered was Dr. Conklin leaning over him on the couch. The doctor explained that Dwight had been unconscious. Dwight's left knee, he said, had become seriously infected.

Dwight was moved from the couch up to his bedroom, where he drifted in and out of consciousness. His mother spent hours each day sitting at his side, and Dr. Conklin visited several times to check Dwight's progress. It was during one of these visits that Dwight, as he lay in a semiconscious state, overheard the doctor tell his mother that the infection was getting worse and that he would have to amputate his leg. Dwight was shocked. Despite how well George Eyser had performed in the Olympic Games with a wooden prosthesis in place of his amputated left leg, Dwight declared that no one was going to amputate his leg. He wouldn't allow it. Dr. Conklin pressured Dwight's parents to give him permission for the amputation and save their son's life, but they refused. They told the doctor they would abide by their son's wishes and that the family would pray for his recovery. Several days later Dwight's fever broke, and the infection began to recede. Dwight was going to recover with both legs intact.

It was two months before Dwight's left leg was strong enough for him to walk without a crutch. By then he'd missed so much school he decided to skip the rest of the year and return to Abilene High School in fall 1905 and redo his ninth-grade year. Around the same time, Edgar announced that he was tired of working menial jobs and wanted to return to school and start ninth grade at Abilene High School. Dwight wasn't sure if he liked this idea or not. He and Edgar had always competed in everything, from who could hit a baseball farther to which of them could balance thirty feet up in the air on the crossbeam of the barn. Now the two of them would be in the same classes and play on the same sports teams for the next four years. Edgar would have the advantage, since he was bigger and stronger and two years older than Dwight.

Chapter 4

A Path Forward

On his first day back at Abilene High School in fall 1905 to repeat ninth grade, Dwight realized his standing in the class had changed. Since Eisenhower was a relatively long name to say, many people in Abilene called Dwight and all his brothers Ike. With Edgar in the same class, Dwight became Little Ike, while Edgar was known by the more impressive nickname Big Ike. Though it was obvious to Dwight that Edgar was bigger and stronger than he was, nonetheless it irked him that his nickname was a reminder to all that he was the smaller, younger brother. He wondered how he and Edgar would get along being in the same class all day every day and then being at home together in the evenings and on weekends.

Dwight and Edgar both progressed through the first half of ninth grade. Then in spring 1906, the school relocated. Abilene's education committee had worked long and hard to raise money to build a new high school on Seventh Street, just east of Garfield School. Once the money was raised, the new school was built, and Abilene High School's teachers and students moved from the town hall to the new location. While Dwight appreciated the new building, the location was nowhere as exciting. There were no fire trucks for the boys to haul to fires in town or prisoners breaking out of jail.

Soon after Dwight moved to the new high school, his grandfather died of a stroke, leaving Dwight with no living grandparents. He missed sitting beside his grandfather on the front porch, listening to stories and the creaking of the rocking chair. Then in September, Dwight's oldest brother, Arthur, married seventeen-year-old Alida Legg, whom he'd met in Kansas City.

While the Eisenhower family was changing, so was Dwight. People began to view Dwight as the natural leader of the brothers who were still at home, even though Edgar was older and more experienced.

Dwight loved any sport but settled on football and baseball as his two favorites. There were many differences between the two sports. The main one was that baseball uniforms and equipment were funded by Abilene High School, but it was not so for football. When Dwight played football, it was often a scramble to get a whole team together. And when they did, the players wore a mishmash of colored sweaters and long pants with newspaper stuffed in the legs for protection. Dwight thought the disparity between baseball and football was unfair and decided that if no one else was going to fix the problem, he would.

In fall 1908—his senior year—Dwight was elected president of the school's newly formed Athletic Association. As president, he set about raising funds for both the football and the baseball teams.

Somehow Dwight managed to balance it all—doing chores at home, getting As and Bs in his schoolwork, playing football and baseball, and raising money for the Athletic Association. His biggest challenge was chairing Athletic Association meetings as members argued over the wording of a constitution Ike insisted they write.

Dwight's senior year at Abilene High School passed swiftly, and at graduation he and Edgar listened as the commencement speaker, the editor of a newspaper in Wichita, Kansas, addressed the class. "I would sooner begin life over again with one arm cut off than attempt to struggle without a college education," the speaker stated. A feeling of hopelessness overcame Dwight. His parents didn't have the money to send him or Edgar to college. Nonetheless, the high school yearbook editor predicted that Edgar would be a future president of the United States while Dwight would become a professor of history at Yale University. Both predictions seemed far-fetched to Dwight, who assumed that he and Edgar would most likely spend the rest of their lives working at the creamery with their father.

After graduation, as Dwight had dreaded, he and Edgar filled their lunch pails early each morning and headed to the Belle Springs Creamery to work alongside their father. As the two brothers talked about leaving high school behind, Dwight realized he preferred the nickname Ike, not Little Ike. Meanwhile, Edgar went back to being called his real name. From then on Dwight asked people to call him Ike.

At the Belle Springs Creamery, Ike worked in the ice-making plant. His job was to produce three-hundred-pound blocks of ice, guide them down a chute with huge metal tongs, and load them into railroad boxcars or onto horse-drawn wagons.

At home in the evenings, Ike and Edgar often discussed their predicament. They were both desperate to go to college, but how? Gradually, they began to form a plan. If they couldn't go to college together, maybe they could take turns going. Since Edgar was two years older, he had a clearer idea of what he wanted to study. They agreed that Edgar would go to college while Ike continued working at the creamery, sending every cent he could spare from his paycheck to help support his brother. The following year the brothers would switch roles, with Ike attending college and Edgar working at the creamery and supporting him. In this way, if everything went according to plan, the two brothers would have their degrees in eight years.

That fall, Edgar used the money he and Ike had saved and set out for the University of Michigan in Ann Arbor, where he planned to work on a law degree. While he studied, back home Ike worked hard and tried to make the most of this new life plan.

By now most of Ike's school friends had also

settled into jobs. Many of them lacked the ambition Ike possessed, and Ike struggled to find people he could talk to about his dream of going to college.

The year passed quickly, and Ike managed to send Edgar $200, which he had eked out of the $60 monthly paycheck from which he also had to pay his parents for room and board. Toward the end of the school year, Edgar wrote to ask Ike if they could change their agreement. He wanted to stay at the University of Michigan to study for one more year while Ike continued to support him. Ike wasn't eager to do this, but he realized it would be easier to earn a degree in two-year bursts rather than in the one-year-on and one-year-off original agreement.

The change in plan seemed dreary to Ike until he was reunited with "Swede" Hazlett. Swede had been a year behind Ike at Abilene High School before being sent off to a study at a military academy in Wisconsin. Swede explained to Ike that his father, a prominent surgeon in town, had decided his son would do better attending a more rigorous high school. Over the summer of 1910, Ike and Swede rekindled their acquaintance and became good friends.

Swede told Ike that he didn't intend stay long in Abilene. He saw his future in either the US Army or the US Navy. In pursuit of that dream he had applied to both the United States Naval Academy in Annapolis, Maryland, and the United States Military Academy in West Point, New York. Swede was accepted to the Naval Academy. However, he had failed the mathematics portion of his entrance exam and was now home to study for a second try at passing it. He asked Ike if he would like to study alongside him.

Suddenly Ike saw a path forward for himself, a faster plan than the one he and Edgar had hatched. He could go to a military training academy and earn a degree with no money out of pocket. It was a brilliant solution—that is, if he could pass the entrance exam and convince a local congressman or senator to recommend him for the post. Ike was sure he could do both things, and soon he and Swede were spending hours together each day studying past Annapolis and West Point entrance exams.

By now Ike had been promoted to boilerman at the creamery. In this new job he worked the night shift, during which he stoked the boilers with coal for about ten minutes every hour and removed the hot ashes that fell through the grate. This left him with plenty of time to study.

In fall 1910, Ike received permission to return to his old high school in the mornings so he could retake classes in mathematics, physics, and chemistry. He'd passed these classes the first time around, but now he wanted to excel in them, and this gave him the opportunity to ask the teachers lots of questions. He continued working nights at the creamery and spent every minute he could studying.

Ike knew that his mother was deeply disappointed that he wanted to join the military. As a devoted member of the International Bible Study movement, she believed a person's loyalty should be to God and not to a man-made government. Despite his mother's misgivings about his plans, Ike was thankful that she didn't openly stand in his way, though he knew she prayed earnestly that he would choose another career.

At the beginning of October 1910, Ike and Swede, along with seven other young men from the state, traveled to Topeka, Kansas, to undertake two days of pretests for the military service academies. Ike already knew his only chance was getting into the Military Academy at West Point. The Naval Academy at Annapolis required that a candidate win a place and enter the academy before his twentieth birthday. Regrettably, Ike would turn twenty years old later that month, missing the cutoff. The exams were tough, and Ike was surprised by the results. He placed first in English but much lower in history and geometry—the two subjects he felt most confident in. Still, his scores were high enough to get him to the next level in the selection process—the actual entrance exams for West Point, which were to be held in January 1911 at Jefferson Barracks in Lemay, Missouri, just south of St. Louis.

Although Dwight had been born in Denison, Texas, he wasn't even two years old when his family had moved back to Abilene, and he remembered nothing of Texas. As far as Dwight was concerned, the four-hundred-mile trip to Jefferson Barracks was his first trip outside Kansas. It was an exciting moment for him. He had listened longingly as Swede told him all about life and the land in Wisconsin and the other states he'd visited, and now Ike would see a new state for himself.

Dwight wished he had more time to take in all

the sights and experiences in Missouri, but he was there for a specific purpose and tried to keep his mind focused on it. The West Point entrance examinations were held over four days and included both written and physical tests. Ike poured his focus and energy into the tests, and at the end of the four days he felt he'd given his best effort. Now he would have to wait and see what the outcome would be.

Several weeks passed as Ike anxiously awaited the result of the entrance exams. He tried focusing on work at the creamery, but it wasn't easy. As he waited, he learned that Swede had passed his exams and gained entry into the United States Naval Academy in Annapolis. Ike was happy for him.

Then one day an official envelope was waiting for Ike when he arrived home from work. With trembling hands he opened the envelope, took out the enclosed letter, unfolded it, and began to read. "You are ordered to report to the United States Military Academy (USMA) at West Point, New York, before noon on June 14, 1911." Ike let out a whoop. He'd made it into the academy. Real adventures awaited him, far from Abilene.

Chapter 5

West Point

Ike sat on the train bound for West Point in New York State. He was on the final leg of his 1,250-mile easterly journey from Abilene, Kansas. It was the farthest he'd ever traveled from home. Along the way he stopped in Chicago to visit an old school friend and then headed to Ann Abor, Michigan, to spend a few days with Edgar. As the train rumbled along, Ike thought about how his path had diverged from Edgar's. His brother appeared to be having a great time at the University of Michigan and had lots of girls chasing him for dates. By contrast, Ike knew that dating was against regulations for United States Military Academy cadets. But while he couldn't date, he reminded himself he was headed to the most prestigious military academy in the country. His main aim, however, was to get an education, not to become a military man. As the train got closer to his final destination, Ike wondered if he'd made the right decision. He would just have to wait and see how things turned out.

Mid-morning on Wednesday, June 14, the train came to a halt at Highland Falls Station. Through the carriage window to the right Ike saw the mighty Hudson River flowing by, and to the left he could see a cliff rimmed with trees. He grabbed his small suitcase and joined other recruits making their way down the aisle and off the train into bright sunlight. Upperclassmen from the military academy stood posted at the station. They yelled, "Pick up your bags and move it!" at the newcomers, whom they referred to as plebes.

Ike joined the throng of young men making their way along the steep path toward the military academy. As he walked, he smiled to himself. He knew he would be called a plebe, the term for first-year cadets, and that he was about to be put through some rough treatment at the hands of the upperclassmen, but he felt ready to handle it. He figured growing up in a family of six boys had prepared him for it, and besides, he was a year or two older than most of the other new cadets. He hoped this would give him the mental edge he needed to push through the initial summer training.

For Ike, the rest of the morning and most of the afternoon was a blur of yelling and running as the yearlings and cows (second- and third-year cadets) ordered the plebes around. Ike weighed in at 150 pounds and measured five feet eleven inches in height for his uniform.

At the end of the day, all 287 newly arrived cadets lined up in full dress uniform on the Plain, the large grassy field at the center of the academy, to take the oath of allegiance and officially become United States Military Academy cadets. As he stood with the other cadets, their right hands raised, Ike thought about his parents. Their religious beliefs forbade them from taking an oath, much less being trained in the art of war, yet here he was, about to embark upon a life of his own choosing. As he took the oath, unexpected emotions welled up within him, and Ike had to remind himself to be practical. He had come to West Point to get an education and play football and baseball. He didn't know how long he would stay in the army after graduating, but that didn't really matter to him. What mattered was that at the end of it all he would have a degree that would serve as his ticket to a good career.

The official swearing-in ceremony marked the beginning of basic training, designed to turn newly arrived West Point plebes from civilians into cadets. The first three weeks of this process was ominously referred to as Beast Barracks. That night Ike met his assigned roommate, Henry Dykes, who hailed from a small town in Kansas. Ike soon discovered that that was about all the two of them had in common. As they lay in their beds, seventeen-year-old Henry described the grand send-off he had received from his hometown. A brass band played as he made his way to the railway station where the residents of the town had gathered to wish him well as he climbed aboard the train headed for West Point.

As he drifted off to sleep thinking about the things his roommate had told him, Ike knew that Henry was going to have difficulty adjusting to his new reality. At home he'd been pampered by his family and the townsfolk. Now he was a raw cadet on the bottom rung of life at West Point. By contrast, Ike knew he had already been toughened for what lay ahead through his fair share of bad bosses and hard knocks.

The next morning the cadets were awakened at dawn to a full day of frenetic activity that started with rigorous physical fitness training. All of the day's activities were carried out under the watchful eye of several hundred upperclassmen whom Ike and the other cadets had to obey. Ike couldn't go more than a few feet without having to stop and salute someone or be told to put his shoulders back and look straight ahead while he walked. When the cadets walked, there was no dawdling allowed. They had to move in double-quick time. Worst of all, Ike discovered he couldn't march in time and was relegated to the "awkward squad" while he learned how to coordinate his feet and arms.

Along with all the physical exercises and marching, during the first half of their basic training the cadets were taught how to adapt themselves to West Point and military life. Here Ike learned how to act, speak, and present himself in a soldierly manner. After that, the new cadets began training in military tactics: how to hold and properly fire military weapons, how to navigate terrain using a compass, and many other skills they needed to have to become successful officers.

Each night, back in his room after another exhausting day of training, Ike would try to keep Henry Dykes's spirits up. "This will end," he repeatedly told his roommate. "Think of how many thousands of cadets have gotten through this before us." Henry would weep at the indignation of constantly being yelled at and told he was useless. Six weeks after arriving, Henry dropped out of West Point. Ike felt sorry for him and once again was thankful he hadn't been coddled growing up. Sometimes he even wanted to laugh when an upperclassman gave him some ridiculous order, but he knew better than to do that.

After the three weeks of Beast Barracks, the new cadets moved down beside the Hudson River where they camped out in tents and continued their training. Ike also got a new tentmate, Paul Hodgson. Paul was also from a small town in Kansas. However, he came from a large, rambunctious family and loved sports. Ike knew the two of them would get along well. Paul was almost a year younger than Ike, and the two immediately began encouraging each other to train hard with the goal of making the Black Knights—the West Point football team—in the fall.

In September, Ike and the other new cadets left their camp on the riverbank and marched back to take up residence in what was called New Barracks, a cold, gray stone barracks located near the gymnasium. It was time for serious study.

In the limited spare time allotted West Point plebes, Ike enjoyed hiking around the academy's campus. He often ended up on the point looking across the Hudson River to Constitution Island, where General George Washington had ordered a gigantic sixty-five-ton iron chain to be strung across the river to stop British ships sailing up into the Hudson Valley, thus dividing the American colonies in two. Fort Putnam, the original fort at West Point, was built to protect the chain and to fire cannons at British ships as they tacked in the narrow channel. In his mind, Ike loved to run through various Revolutionary War battles fought in the vicinity, critiquing each side's strengths and weaknesses as he did so.

As the weeks passed, Ike adjusted to life and the routine at West Point. He was a popular class member who was always up for a practical joke, but he was dead serious about earning a position on the Black Knights football team. Since he and Paul were the same height and weight, they competed fiercely, trying to outdo each other in gaining weight.

Their friendly competition paid off. By the time the team tryouts began in fall, both men weighed 170 pounds. Ike gave the tryouts his all, but when the lineup was announced, he learned he hadn't made the team, though Paul had. It was a setback for Ike, but after the initial discouragement he reminded himself he was only a plebe and had three more years to make the team. He set even higher fitness goals for himself and kept going.

In October, when Ike turned twenty-one, he received a letter from his mother saying his brother

Edgar was planning to marry Louise Alexander the following month. Although he and Edgar were only twenty-three months apart in age and had always been competitive, Ike was happy to let his brother win this competition. He couldn't imagine getting married himself.

At Christmas, the plebes with excellent disciplinary records were permitted eight days' leave. For Ike, however, his practical jokes and lackadaisical attitude toward being on time for class meant he had to stay behind at West Point. He wasn't too concerned. He wouldn't have had enough time to make the train trip to Kansas and back anyhow. Instead, Ike enjoyed the extra time roaming the academy campus and the hills around it.

The year 1912 started off well for Ike, who was determined to make the football team. He already had an assurance that if he could reform his "chopping" action while swinging at the baseball he had a good chance of making the baseball team too. Ike's hard work paid off, and in the fall tryouts he was chosen to be a member of the Black Knights football team.

On November 16, 1912, the Black Knights played a game against the Tufts University team. During one play in the second half of the game, as Ike surged through the defensive line, a player managed to get a hand on his foot. As Ike shifted his weight and struggled to get free of his opponent's grip, he twisted his right knee badly. He felt no pain at the time, but his knee instantly began to swell. The injury forced him to leave the game, and he was taken to the infirmary, where he spent four days recovering. When released from the infirmary, he had to walk with crutches to get around, forcing Ike to miss the Navy game, which he had been anticipating playing in. After some time he was able to set the crutches aside and walk without them.

Several days after walking without crutches, Ike reported to the riding hall to practice mounting and dismounting a horse. During practice, his horse reared, sending Ike flying. He landed on his right leg as he came down, and Ike felt a searing pain jolt through his body. Once more he was sent to the infirmary, where he learned he'd dislocated his knee and torn the ligaments holding it in place. According to the doctor, he was in for a long, painful recovery. And worse, when his knee did heal, he would no long be able to play sports. The knee would be problematic for the rest of his life.

The news depressed Ike. Nothing mattered to him more than playing sports, and now with a football tackle and a fall from a horse, it was all over. From now on he would be a sports spectator instead of a player. He began to question the purpose of being at West Point. He had nothing to focus on, nothing to train for. Watching other cadets play sports while he sat on the sidelines had never been Ike's way. He liked to be right in the middle of things. He wanted to leave West Point, but friends talked him out of it. He deliberately began breaking rules and shrugging off the consequences. Cadets were allowed to smoke cigars or pipes, but cigarettes were strictly forbidden, so Ike took up smoking them. Avoiding detection while smoking became a game to him.

As he dealt with his disappointment, Ike continued his studies. He enjoyed some classes more than others. His favorite classes always involved studying and arguing over specific battle strategies. It took his mind back to 1904, when he had placed a world map on his bedroom wall in Abilene and tracked the movements of armies in the Russo-Japanese War with pushpins.

Now, ten years later, another war was beginning. In late July and early August 1914, Europe erupted in battle as Germany and the Austro-Hungarian Empire declared war on Russia, France, and Belgium. In response, on August 4, Great Britain declared war on Germany, and on August 12 the British and the French declared war on the Austro-Hungarians. Ike and Paul eagerly followed every scrap of information they could lay their hands on. Once again Ike pinned a map on the wall in his room and tracked troop movements.

With the advent of war in Europe, President Woodrow Wilson thought the United States should stay out of it and try to broker a peace agreement. He also tried to foster trade with both sides in the conflict. But when the British imposed a naval blockade on Germany, the president eventually agreed to it. Germany responded to the blockade by launching sustained submarine attacks against merchant ships around the British Isles.

As 1915, his final year at West Point, rolled along, Ike wondered where he might be assigned after graduation. He realized that many of the newly graduated officers would be sent south to the

US-Mexico border, where tensions were rising by the day. Because that didn't sound like much of an adventure, Ike requested the Philippines. As far as he knew he was the only cadet to do so, which gave him high odds of receiving his choice.

In May 1915, as graduation loomed, a German submarine torpedoed and sank the British ocean liner RMS *Lusitania*, killing 1,198 passengers and crew, including 128 American citizens. In response, Woodrow Wilson protested to the Germans, demanding they take immediate steps to ensure that another incident like the sinking of the *Lusitania* would never happen again.

At West Point, Colonel Shaw, the academy's chief medical officer, called Ike to his office to discuss his knee injury. While he could walk, run, and do physical exercises, the injury still bothered Ike a lot, especially since the knee would give out on him at unexpected moments. Colonel Shaw had stern words for Ike. After reviewing his medical record, he said he didn't think the army wanted to keep Ike. Ike really didn't care. He'd come to West Point for a free education and would be leaving with one. He told the colonel not to feel bad for him. Colonel Shaw looked incredulous. "Are you sure you're going to be all right with that?" he asked. Ike smiled, "Yes, sir. I might even go to Argentina and spend a few years there. I've read about it. It sounds like the Wild West."

Ike left Colonel Shaw's office and ordered some brochures on travel to South America. A few days later, Colonel Shaw called Ike back to his office. This time he described what he thought was good news for Ike. "I've been going over your case, and I've read your entire record. You can't ride a horse again, so the cavalry is out, but if you request the Coastal Artillery Corps, I think I could sign off on that."

Ike nearly jumped out of his chair. "The CAC?" He couldn't think of anything less adventurous than polishing fixed guns in some remote US coastal location. The men who joined the CAC, as the Coastal Artillery Corps was known, were made fun of for avoiding real army work. "Well, how about the infantry? I've always wanted to join the infantry," Ike blurted out, not even thinking through what he was saying.

Colonel Shaw looked at Ike quizzically. "If you're sure, and you agree to stay there for the rest of your career in the army, I think I could recommend you for that," he said.

Ike left the colonel's office, unsure of what had just happened. He was going to be in the infantry. Was that what he wanted? Wouldn't it be better to have taken the discharge and gone to Argentina? Ike didn't know quite what to do.

For the remainder of his time at West Point, Ike did what was necessary to pass his classes and not much more. He clocked up a total of 307 demerit points for everything from being late for class and meals to being absent for room inspection. Thankfully, the academy's commanding officer never found out about some of his worst escapades. A cadet could be sent home for leaving West Point without permission, but Ike regularly led a group of friends who climbed out a bathroom window, sneaked past the sentry guard, and hired a boat to row fifteen miles up the Hudson River to Newburgh for a snack. Such escapades provided him with a constant flow of stories with which to regale his classmates.

On June 12, 1915, Ike stood proudly at attention with the 164 cadets who were graduating and being commissioned as second lieutenants in the US Army. Ike placed sixty-first out of the 164 cadets who made it through the four-year program. He was aware that his superior officers had wildly varying opinions of him. Some told him he was too impulsive and would never get far in the army, while others said they could clearly see the markers for future leadership.

At twenty-four years of age, Second Lieutenant Dwight Eisenhower had made it through the most elite army academy in the United States. He had his degree. Now it was time for him to go home, take a break, and await his commission to the Philippines.

Chapter 6

Mamie

Fort Sam Houston, Texas!" Ike exclaimed aloud to himself as he read the letter. "They're sending me to Texas?" He read the letter twice, just to make sure he hadn't made a mistake. He'd hoped his commission after graduating from the United States Military Academy at West Point would be a ticket to see the world. But instead of the Philippines, which he'd requested, he had been assigned to a military base just eight hundred miles south of where he grew up.

Ike was disappointed, but after some soul-searching he decided to accept the assignment. He would go to Fort Sam Houston and be the best soldier he could be—not a soldier who attracted attention, but a solid, hard worker who tried his best to follow orders. With this mindset, in mid-September 1915 Ike packed his bag and boarded a train that would carry him south from his home in Abilene, Kansas to join the 19th Infantry as a second lieutenant.

Upon arrival at Fort Sam Houston, Ike was allocated a suite of two small rooms in the bachelor quarters, where he stowed his few belongings and set out to explore the base. He already knew that the fort, like West Point, had an interesting history. It had been established in the 1870s with a grant of forty acres from the city of San Antonio. In 1886, Geronimo, Chief Natchez, and their band of Apaches had surrendered to US Army forces at this fort. And more recently, Teddy Roosevelt had assembled his Rough Riders at Fort Sam, as the place was affectionately known, before they set off to participate in the invasion of Cuba.

Upon reporting for duty, Ike was assigned to take charge of the mess hall. Most officers in this position focused on making sure the pots and pans were sparkling clean and that the place was neat and tidy. But Ike went further. He remembered the lessons his mother had taught him in the kitchen growing up and often questioned the cooks on how they prepared the food.

It took Ike only a few days to settle in to life at Fort Sam Houston. Following four years of intense study at West Point, he discovered that he now had more spare time on his hands. Army officers typically worked until mid-afternoon, when they took time out to participate in all kinds of sports for the rest of the day and into the evening. While Ike would have loved to participate, his knee dislocated easily, so he had to be content to watch from the sidelines.

On Sunday afternoon, October 17, 1915, three days after his twenty-fifth birthday, Ike was named officer of the day. He was about to begin his rounds of the fort, a three-mile circuit on which he checked to make sure that everything was safe and secure. His sidearm strapped to his belt, he stepped out from his bachelor quarters into the sunlight. He heard a woman's voice call to him. "Come over here, Lieutenant Eisenhower."

Ike looked in the direction of the voice and recognized Lulu Harris, a fellow officer's wife, sitting on the porch of the married couple's barracks. Several civilians were with her. "I have to start my inspection round," he replied politely.

"I'm not asking you to come over here to stay, just to meet some friends of mine," Lulu said.

With a nod, Ike walked over to the porch, where he was introduced to, among others, Mamie Doud, a vivacious young woman whom Ike liked immediately, so much so he asked her if she would like to walk with him as he made his inspection round. She agreed, and the two started off together.

As they walked around Fort Sam Houston, Ike caught a glimpse of just how different their lives were. Mamie's father, John Doud, was a wealthy man who'd owned a meatpacking business in Colorado, made enough money to support his family, and retired at age forty. Mamie had two younger sisters: Eda, age fifteen, and thirteen-year-old Mable. Her father had wanted sons and so nicknamed his two youngest daughters Buster and Mike. The Doud family spent summers in Denver and winters in San

Antonio. The household employed four servants and always sent two of them ahead by train to prepare the house, while the other two servants drove with the family between their two homes in their seven-seat touring car.

By contrast, the Eisenhowers had never owned a car, and Ike's father planned on working until he died. Ike found it hard to wrap his mind around the luxury and expense of owning homes in two states.

By the time he'd completed his inspection round, Ike was intrigued by Mamie Doud. As if her petite frame, bright blue eyes, short, bobbed brunette hair, and impish smile were not enough, she liked to dance and go to parties.

Over the next few months, Ike learned a lot more about Mamie. She turned nineteen years old on November 14, 1915, and had an older sister, Eleanor, who had died as a result of a heart condition three and a half years before, leaving the Doud family devastated. For a variety of reasons, Mamie had been in and out of school most of her life, though her parents had insisted she attend Miss Wolcott School for Girls in Denver during the past year. Having finished school, Mamie was now being officially introduced to society.

When Ike asked if he could see more of Mamie, she explained she already had a long procession of young men who had reserved dates with her. But Ike wasn't deterred. He visited the Doud home on fashionable McCullough Avenue. If Mamie was not at home, he would visit with her parents, John and

Elvira, or joke around with her two younger sisters. The more time he spent with the Douds, the more Ike discovered he liked the entire family. Elvira Doud was a first-generation American who'd emigrated from Sweden. In many ways the Douds were the opposite of the Eisenhowers. They were an all-girl family, while Ike had been raised in an all-boy family. The Doud girls whispered secrets and showed affection to each other. They spent endless hours together, poring over issues of *Vogue* magazine and comparing ruffled blouses and wide-brimmed hats. Every birthday and holiday in the family was meticulously planned and celebrated. No detail was too small a matter.

Mamie's father, John, doted on his daughters. He was a shrewd businessman who loved discussing politics and history, and there was always information on the Great War taking place in Europe to dissect. John and Ike talked of the disastrous Gallipoli campaign, where Great Britain and her allies seemed to be losing the fight to wrestle control of the Gallipoli Peninsula and the strait that linked the Aegean Sea to the Black Sea from the Ottoman Empire. The two men spoke of how the Germans had developed a synchronized machine gun that could be mounted on airplanes and fire bullets between the propeller blades.

As fall turned into winter, Mamie at last agreed to go on a date with Ike. He spent more than he could afford of his $142 monthly paycheck on a lavish dinner at St. Anthony Hotel and a show at the

Majestic Theater. More date nights followed, though with modest dinners at a local Tex-Mex restaurant and dancing.

The romance between Ike and Mamie progressed quickly. On February 14, 1916—Valentine's Day—Ike gave Mamie his West Point class ring and asked her to marry him. She said yes, but her father was not so sure about the idea. He pointed out to Ike that Mamie was only nineteen years old and less than a year out of school. Not only that, she was used to having everything she wanted—shopping sprees in New York City and servants to cook her meals and clean for her. John Doud asked how Ike thought his daughter would cope living on his meager income, and John made it clear he would not be giving her an allowance as a married woman.

Mamie convinced Ike she didn't care about any of those things. They would find a way forward together. Their love was stronger than any hardships they might face. After many conversations, Mamie's father agreed to let the two of them marry when she turned twenty in November 1916.

As spring approached, the Doud family prepared to return to Denver for the summer. Mamie went with them to set everything up for her November wedding there. Just before she left, Ike gave her a proper engagement ring, which he had bought with money borrowed from his father.

Things did not go as planned. For a number of years, tension between Mexico and the United States had been building. One after another a succession of Mexican governments failed, and with the collapse of each government, border conditions deteriorated. As 1916 rolled along, charismatic Mexican renegade Pancho Villa and his band of pistoleros launched a string of violent attacks along the US-Mexico border. Americans at the border were kidnapped or killed, and small towns were attacked, looted, and burned. At the same time the latest Mexican government appeared to be on the verge of collapse. Mexico seemed to have become a lawless and ungovernable place. In response, more US soldiers were stationed along the border in Texas and New Mexico. As well, President Woodrow Wilson lost his patience with Mexico, and the War Department began planning a punitive attack on the country in retaliation for Pancho Villa's attacks on American people and property along the border. Ike hoped to join the attack on Mexico, which was to be led by General John Pershing.

Given the changed circumstances, Ike felt the need to move up his wedding to Mamie lest he be sent to Mexico to fight before their planned November date. He talked to Mamie about the situation, and she agreed they should marry sooner and then convinced her parents to accept a change of plan. At noon on Saturday, July 1, 1916, Ike and Mamie Geneva Doud were married in a small ceremony at the Doud home in Denver. Ike had been able to secure ten days of leave to travel to Colorado for the wedding. After a short honeymoon at a cabin in nearby Eldorado Springs, on July 6 Ike and Mamie boarded the train to Abilene so that Ike could introduce his new bride to his parents and family.

The train departed Denver at five o'clock in the afternoon and pulled into Abilene at three o'clock the following morning. David Eisenhower, Ike's father, was waiting for them at the railway station when they disembarked. When they reached the Eisenhower home, Ike's mother, Ida, was at the front door. After Mamie was introduced to the family, they all talked until sunrise as Ike caught up on news of all his brothers. Edgar and Louise had settled in Tacoma, Washington, and their baby son, Merrill, was a healthy child. Roy was about to head off to college to study pharmacy, and the two younger boys, Earl and Milton, were both excelling at school. Ike also learned that after twenty-four years his father had quit his job at the creamery and taken a new job managing the local gas plant. His father was now in his fifties, and Ike was grateful he would be doing less backbreaking labor in the new position. Even so, he knew his father would be earning less than Ike did as a second lieutenant in the army.

Ida Eisenhower prepared a big breakfast that included fried chicken and apple strudel for them all to enjoy. It was the best meal Ike had eaten in a while. Mamie did her best to fit in with the Eisenhowers, but Ike could tell from the expressions on her face she'd never been in a home like his. After breakfast, Ike and Mamie headed back to the railway station to catch another train at eleven that morning.

From Abilene, Ike and Mamie traveled to Kansas City, where they stopped for a few hours to visit with Ike's oldest brother, Arthur, and his wife, Alida, before boarding the train for the final leg of their journey back to San Antonio.

The trip from Kansas City to San Antonio was long and hot. Ike and Mamie alternately napped and talked. Mamie explained she could hardly believe his mother and two youngest brothers did all their own cooking, sewing, and gardening. It hardly seemed possible to her they could do that much work in a day without the help of a maid. Moreover, she realized they didn't smoke, gamble, or dance, and she asked Ike if they had any fun at all. Ike laughed. He'd had plenty of fun growing up—camping with Bob Davis, wrestling his brothers, and jumping off the railway bridge during summer into the river below. It was all just a very different kind of fun than what Mamie and her sisters had experienced.

When Ike and Mamie arrived at Fort Sam Houston, they learned some good news and some bad news. On his wedding day, Ike had been promoted to the rank of first lieutenant, which came with a $20 a month pay increase. However, there were no married couple apartments available for them to move into, and they would have to cram themselves into Ike's two-room bachelor quarters.

Mamie set out to make the two rooms into a home. She rented a piano for $5 a month. It took up half the living room. Ike smiled to himself. That was one thing Mamie and his mother had in common—they would forego just about any other piece of furniture for a piano. Since Mamie didn't see how she could live without an icebox either, they bought one and put it in the bathroom.

As part of their wedding present, Mamie's father gave them an automobile, a Pullman Roadster. The vehicle arrived in San Antonio strapped down on a flatbed railcar.

It didn't take long before Ike realized just how pampered Mamie had been during her life. She was used to servants and had never made her own bed, let alone scrubbed a floor or cooked a meal. She told Ike her mother had always said, "If you don't learn how to cook, no one will ask you to do it."

At first Ike was amused by just how little his new wife knew about how to run a home—even a two-room one—but frustration soon set in. They ate their dinners at the officers' club, but Ike's meager income didn't stretch far now that two people were living off it. Besides purchasing extra food, Ike now had to buy ice for the icebox and gasoline for the car, pay rent for the piano, and supply Mamie with pocket money. Something had to change.

After a few difficult conversations, Mamie agreed to let Ike teach her how to cook simple meals like beans and rice. She also took over managing their money, which made her more aware of how much they were spending. Slowly she began to get better control of their finances.

Despite their money struggles, the Eisenhowers loved to entertain. They played cards with other couples or had musical evenings where Mamie belted out the latest tunes on the piano. Their two-room quarters soon became known as Club Eisenhower.

In the fall, Mamie's parents and sisters made the

usual long drive from Denver to San Antonio. Ike was glad to see them. He liked their jovial ways, and Mamie was happy to see her sisters.

On November 7, 1916, the United States held a presidential election in which Woodrow Wilson won a second term as president by promising to keep the country out of the war still raging in Europe.

Christmas came and went, and at the end of December Mamie learned she was pregnant. She would complain when Ike left her for any length of time, but he always reminded her that his duty to his country would always come first and that she would need to adjust to being an army officer's wife.

At the same time, Ike began adjusting to the idea that the United States would join Great Britain and her Allies in the war in Europe. On February 1, 1917, the Germans violated the agreement they had with the United States to leave American ships alone. They began torpedoing them from their submarines.

Ike wished he had a radio so he could follow the events of the war more closely. Since he could not afford one, he had to rely on newspapers to stay informed. About a month after the Germans began attacking American ships, he read in the newspaper how British Intelligence had intercepted and decrypted messages sent from German Foreign Minister Arthur Zimmermann to the German ambassador in Mexico City. In these messages the German government promised to help Mexico recover territory it had ceded to the United States following the Mexican-American War. In return, the German

Foreign Minister asked for Mexico's support in their war.

With such a revelation, Ike knew American involvement in the war must be only weeks away, regardless of what the president said. Sure enough, on April 2, 1917, President Wilson went before a joint session of Congress to request a declaration of war against Germany. By April 6, the United States Senate and House of Representatives had both voted in support of the measure to declare war on Germany.

It was a sobering moment for all. Ike was confident he would be heading to France soon to fight on the war's western front, leaving behind a wife and soon-to-be-born baby.

Chapter 7

Tank Corps

Within days, Ike received his orders. He was to join the 57th Infantry, a brand-new regiment, as the supply officer. Ike gulped hard as his commanding officer, Colonel D. J. Baker, described what the position would entail. President Wilson had ordered that eight new military camps be established in the United States to train officers for combat leadership. Colonel Baker explained that the first of these new First Officers Training Camps (FOTC), Camp Wilson, would be run by the 57th Infantry.

"We don't have much time to prepare," he continued. "In one week three thousand army recruits will arrive, wearing their uniforms and carrying barracks bags. That's it. You'll be responsible for giving them supper the night they arrive. From the next morning on, you'll be expected to supply them all with shelter, food, stoves, latrines, medicines, fighting equipment, and anything else they need to make their training successful."

Ike's mind raced. *Three thousand new recruits*? That meant supplying nine thousand meals each day and over 350 tents for the recruits to sleep in, along with a field hospital, motor vehicles, office equipment . . . the list went on and on. For the next five days Ike was busy meeting with anyone he thought might be able to help him. Thankfully, he had one officer with supply experience on his team. Together they wrote list after list of what they needed, and soon some of the necessary equipment arrived at Fort Sam. Ike then had to borrow trucks to transport it to the new camp site adjacent to Fort Sam Houston.

Once the trucks delivered the equipment necessary to build the Camp Wilson tent city, Ike's new enemy became the soil, a mix of gravel and red clay that turned into sticky mud after every rain shower. The work was backbreaking as newly arrived recruits began digging latrines and setting up camp. As soon as the canteens were established and running, the smell of cooking food attracted dark clouds of flies that engulfed the camp. They came from the remount station, Fort Sam's stables, located nearby.

Within weeks, Colonel Baker gave the order to break camp and relocate the FOTC onto land the US government owned at Leon Springs. The new site was twenty miles northwest of Fort Sam Houston and far away from the relentless swarm of flies.

At the new site, Ike was faced with seventeen thousand acres of ranchland without a single building on it. Since 1906 the place had been used as a rifle range and for large-scale maneuvers for Fort Sam soldiers. Now the area needed to be transformed into a training camp for officers. A tent city was laid out, and once again Ike and his team got to work setting up the newly named Camp Funston.

In record time, the First Officers Training Camp was up and running. New recruits were pushed to their limits with practice marches, target shooting practice, and trench warfare training. Everyone worked so hard that Colonel Baker made a rare exception and ordered the camp to take Sundays off.

Only twenty miles separated Ike from Mamie on Sundays, but often there was no camp vehicle going to Fort Sam Houston and back that Ike could hitch a ride on. Early one Sunday morning Ike received a phone call from Mamie. She'd had enough. If Ike was unable to find a way to visit her, she was going to drive their Pullman Roadster out to visit him, and she was leaving Fort Sam in ten minutes. Ike was shocked. Mamie had never before driven a gasoline-powered motorcar with gears. Ike tried to talk her out of it, but Mamie had made up her mind. She was driving to see her husband. Ike agreed to meet her at the entrance to Camp Funston.

Ike walked the mile to the camp gate on Fredericksburg Road and waited anxiously, hoping his pregnant wife was safe. Two hours passed, and then he heard the distant sound of an automobile. Several moments later Mamie came into view, seated behind the steering wheel of the Pullman. As she came closer, she waved her hand and motioned for Ike to jump on the running board of the roadster. She yelled to him that she didn't know how to use the brakes. Ike stepped forward and leaped as the car went by him. He landed safely and firmly on the running board, then slid into the seat beside his wife and applied the brakes, bringing the roadster to a halt. Mamie explained that a sergeant at Fort Sam Houston had started the car for her and quickly shown her how to drive it before pointing her in the direction of Camp Funston. However, the sergeant had forgotten to show her how to change gears and use the brakes to slow the vehicle. Ike was amazed that his wife had made it.

Graduation day for the First Officers Training Camp took place on Wednesday, August 15, 1917. Of the 3,000 recruits, 1,846 had made it through the intense three-month training and were awarded the rank of second lieutenant. Having completed their officer training assignment, the 57th Regiment was divided in two. Half of the men were to be sent across the Atlantic Ocean to France to fight in the war. The other half were to go to Fort Oglethorpe, Georgia, to train another group of officer recruits and conduct battleground simulations. Ike had worked hard and expected to be sent to France. As far as he was concerned, that was where he belonged. He'd spent four years at West Point training to be an army officer, and now, like so many of his West Point classmates, he needed to be at the front lines of the battle leading men in the fight. But to his dismay, he was sent off to Fort Oglethorpe to be involved in another intense three months of training second lieutenants.

Ike was granted a few days' leave before reporting for duty at Fort Oglethorpe. He headed straight back to Fort Sam Houston to spend time with Mamie. He could stay with her for only forty-eight hours before beginning the trip to Georgia. It was difficult for him to leave, knowing their baby would soon be born. The infirmary at Fort Sam had no maternity ward, and Mamie was worried about having to make do with whatever the medical personnel there could manage. She was glad her mother was on her way to San Antonio from Denver to be with her for the remainder of her pregnancy and the birth. His mother-in-law's coming to stay was about the only thing Ike was grateful for as he boarded the train to Chattanooga, Tennessee. Fort Oglethorpe sat south of Chattanooga, across the Georgia state line.

After arriving to take up his new assignment at Fort Oglethorpe, Ike set to work constructing a miniature Western Front battleground, complete with dugouts, trenches, and a large area of no-man's-land across which the recruits would have to find their way. To make his simulation as realistic as possible, he spent time reading up on every detail he could find about what was happening on the battlefront in France.

On September 26, 1917, Ike completed oversight of a lengthy battleground simulation exercise and returned to Fort Oglethorpe headquarters. A telegram awaited him, informing him that Mamie had given birth to a baby boy two days before. The new baby had been named Doud Dwight Eisenhower. Ike was elated. He had a son! He looked forward to meeting him.

In February 1918, Ike at last received the news he'd been waiting for. He was ordered to report to the 65th Engineers at Camp Meade, Maryland, where he was to help with the setup of the 301st Tank Battalion. This new battalion would be deploying to France in the spring. Ike was overjoyed. Tanks were a recent British invention and had been used for less than two years in the fighting in France. The year before, they had broken through the German lines in the French town of Cambrai. With the right infantry support, the Allies were convinced that tanks could help them win the war quickly.

Before reporting to Camp Meade, Ike was able to make a detour to Fort Sam Houston to visit Mamie and Doud Dwight, or Ikky, as Mamie had nicknamed him. Ike had seen his son only once, on a brief Christmas visit to Fort Sam. By now Ikky was five months old. After two enjoyable days with his wife and new son, Ike departed for Camp Meade, wondering when he'd see them again. He expected to be shipped off to fight in France very soon.

Within weeks of arriving at Camp Meade, Ike's hopes of an overseas assignment turned to dust. His commanding officer, Colonel Welborn, told Ike he was so impressed with his superior organizational skills that he wouldn't be deployed to France after all. Instead, the colonel ordered Ike to Camp Colt on the old Civil War battle site at Gettysburg, Pennsylvania. Ike's assignment was to take charge of the army's new Tank Corps training and marshaling center. The 301st Tank Battalion sailed for France without Ike.

By the time Ike reached Gettysburg, on March 15, 1918, his mood was not good. And what he found at Camp Colt didn't cheer him up. Hundreds of empty wooden buildings were situated on the grounds of the camp, along with mess halls, latrines, and warehouses that had all been used in the training of regular troops the year before. Most of the buildings had no windows or floors, and Ike was glad that Colonel Welborn had told him the camp would be open only through summer. It was not a suitable place for soldiers to live during frigid Pennsylvania winters.

At Camp Colt, Ike hired fifty local carpenters to install floors and windows in many of the buildings, and soon troops began rolling into camp. Ike's job was to teach them how to operate a tank and use it effectively in warfare. But there was one problem: no one in the United States had ever built one. Since only the French and British were manufacturing tanks, Ike repeatedly wrote to the War Department asking them to send one from Europe to the camp. In the meantime, he had to improvise. Two soldiers from Brooklyn, New York, volunteered to make mock-up tanks out of old car chassis while they waited for a real tank to materialize.

Once settled at Camp Colt, Ike received permission for Mamie and Ikky to join him there. However, they arrived in April during a very late snowstorm. Ike was busy buying up every heater he could find and moving most of his men into the large mess halls to keep them warm. Because there were now so many men at Fort Colt, accommodation was hard to find for his family. In the end Ike rented a dilapidated four-room house with no electricity. It was the best he could find.

When Mamie saw the place, she was horrified. It smelled dank and had obviously not been lived in for a long time. Since there was no electricity, the only heat source in the place was a potbelly stove, something Mamie had never encountered. To make matters worse, Ikky was running a fever, and came down with chicken pox the following day. It was not the happy reunion Ike had hoped for, and he resolved to find them a better place to live as soon as possible. Two months later they were able to move into an empty fraternity house at Gettysburg College. It was spacious but had no kitchen. Mamie had to wash the dishes in the bathtub.

Once Mamie and Ikky had moved into the bigger place, Mamie's father and sister Buster (Eda) drove out to visit them from Denver. Ike was glad to see them. He enjoyed his father-in-law's company and knew that Buster would be a great help to Mamie.

It was a beautiful day in June when a real tank arrived by train. It was unloaded and driven through Gettysburg to Camp Colt. So many townspeople came to see the tank that Ike had it parked near the camp's gate so curious onlookers could get a close-up view.

The new arrival was a French Renault FT-17. Ike had read all he could about it and was glad to have the opportunity to study it up close. The tank had a gun turret fitted with a 37-millimeter cannon that could rotate 360 degrees, and the vehicle had a top speed of six miles per hour. The tank held two men—the driver in front and the tank commander behind. Inside, the engine was so noisy the two men couldn't hear each other talk, so the tank commander used his feet to kick the driver in various spots to tell him what to do next.

As summer 1918 progressed, more troops poured into Camp Colt for tank training. By mid-July over ten thousand enlisted men and six hundred officers were under Ike's command. The extra men were housed in converted horse stables previously used by the cavalry, since military leaders were predicting that tanks would replace horses and riders.

On September 1, Mamie's father and sister left to return to Denver, and Ike began work on relocating his men farther south for the winter. However, he soon had something much more urgent to deal with.

Nine days later, on September 10, 1918, 124 draftees arrived at Camp Colt for training from Fort Devens, Massachusetts. Following the men's arrival, Lieutenant Colonel Thomas Scott, Camp Colt's chief surgeon, reported to Ike that many of them were feeling achy or suffering from headaches. He explained that all the new arrivals had received a typhoid vaccination before getting on the train to Gettysburg. The lieutenant colonel assumed they would all feel better the next day. But that was not the case. The next morning hundreds of soldiers were sick, and at the field hospital Lieutenant Colonel Scott and his medical staff scrambled to understand what was going on.

By noon they had an answer—Spanish flu. Lieutenant Colonel Scott told Ike he assumed the illness had been brought back to Fort Devens by soldiers returning from fighting in Europe, who had passed it on to the new draftees. Apparently not much was known about the Spanish flu other than that it spread easily and could kill quickly.

Ike sprang into action, determined to do everything he could to contain the outbreak. He talked more with the chief surgeon, who said he assumed everyone at Camp Colt had been exposed to the Spanish flu by now. In response, Ike ordered more tents be pitched on the parade ground, and soldiers were assigned three or four to a tent. The men were to be examined daily by medical personnel, and anyone showing symptoms was to be given his own tent when possible. Ike quarantined the entire camp, placing military police officers at the gate to prevent anyone from leaving without permission.

The local Catholic church at Gettysburg offered Ike the use of their hall to house the most seriously ill patients. The town residents banded together to collect cots and bedding to equip the hall. Orderlies swabbed the hall's floor daily with Lysol or kerosene. Despite their best efforts, within a week, over 145 soldiers from Camp Colt were dead, and a third of the men housed at the camp were ill in bed. The thing that frightened Ike the most about this Spanish flu was the speed with which it killed people. A fit, young private could look well at reveille in the morning and be dead in the makeshift morgue by dinnertime.

The War Department informed Ike that Fort Devens and Camp Colt were two of the first locations in the United States to get the Spanish flu, though it was beginning to spread rapidly across the country. Ike and Mamie spent Ikky's first birthday on September 24 with their stomachs knotted with worry that their son might catch the flu.

Three weeks after the draftees arrived from Fort Devens, the worst of the Spanish flu outbreak seemed at last to be over. The War Department congratulated Ike and Lieutenant Colonel Scott on the way they had handled the illness and requested the chief surgeon and doctors from Camp Colt brief them on how they had been so effective.

On October 14, 1918, Ike turned twenty-eight years old. It was a birthday he would never forget. On that day Colonel Welborn promoted him to the rank of lieutenant colonel for his efforts at quickly containing the Spanish flu outbreak at Camp Colt. Better yet, Ike was ordered to report to Camp Dix in New Jersey on November 18 in preparation for embarkation to France, where he would take command of a tank unit in the fighting. On September 26 a major new push against the Germans had begun at the Western Front, and Ike looked forward to becoming a part of it.

Following the disruption of the Spanish flu outbreak, Ike had planned on spending his last few weeks before going to France finalizing the plans he'd been working on to move the men from Camp Colt to a new, warmer winter location. However, on November 9, 1918, his plans were interrupted by a devastating telegram from his father-in-law. Buster, Mamie's seventeen-year-old sister who'd visited them over the summer, had died from a fast-spreading kidney infection. Mamie and Ike were heartbroken at the news and concerned for Mamie's parents. The Douds had had four daughters, and now only two of them were still living.

The following day Ike accompanied Mamie and Ikky to Harrisburg, Pennsylvania, where he helped his wife and young son board the overnight train to Chicago. From there they would travel on to Denver. Ike's heart ached for Mamie as he kissed her good-bye. He didn't know if or when they would ever see each other again, and he knew that Buster's death had burdened his twenty-one-year-old wife with grief almost too much for her to bear. He hoped she would find comfort in Denver and that Ikky would bring some joy to his grandparents.

The next day, November 11, 1918, regular radio broadcasts were interrupted with news that the war in Europe was over. At five o'clock French time that morning, Germany had signed an armistice agreement with the Allies in a railroad car outside Compiègne.

Ike was in no mood to celebrate upon hearing the news. He was still shocked at how many men he'd lost to the Spanish flu and by the death of his sister-in-law. And now his chance of proving himself as a military leader on the battlefield had evaporated. There would be no deployment to France, no chance to see a tank operating under war conditions, and no opportunity to test all the knowledge he had gained regarding tank warfare.

The war was over, and Ike imagined himself attending West Point reunions. He was probably the only member of his class who had sat out the war within the safety of the United States, the only one with nothing to say when asked to recount his bravest moment in the fighting. Opportunity had passed him by. He would likely spend the rest of his military life at a desk job, if he stayed in the army at all.

Chapter 8

Instant Friends

It didn't take Ike long to realize there was nothing more depressing than being in charge of demobilizing a military camp. Loads of paperwork had to be filled out for each enlisted man. List after list of government inventory had to be made, along with logistics on where and to whom it should go and when they could expect it to arrive. Ike always paid attention to such details, but it was hard for him to stave off depression, especially since Mamie and Ikky were so far away.

By May 1919, 95 percent of the men who'd been part of the Tank Corps had been discharged, and Ike was assigned to Camp Meade, Maryland, while the US government questioned what future role tanks would play in warfare. Ike felt strongly they would play a pivotal part in the army, but many people higher up in the military and government weren't so sure. This left Ike debating whether he should take up a civilian job he had been offered in Indiana. As he debated with himself, a memo crossed his desk announcing that the army was embarking on a grand road trip from one side of the United States to the other. The 3,200-mile road trip on the Old Lincoln Highway was to be part publicity stunt, part opportunity to thank thousands of people in small towns across the country who had sacrificed men in the war, and part large-scale vehicle trial over some of the worst roads in America.

Having grown up in Kansas, Ike knew that roads, especially paved ones, had existed only in or near large towns and cities. As they led out of town, those roads quickly turned into rutted, muddy tracks before disappearing altogether. Even now in 1919, things weren't much better. There were still towns in the west where the long, straight ribbons of railway track that bisected the landscape were the only thing that connected people and freight.

During the war in Europe, the Allies had developed and used new motorized technology such as trucks and vans to help them move men and equipment more efficiently. Because they learned as they went, many mistakes and miscalculations were made. Now that the war was over, the War Department thought it was time to work out which makes of cars, vans, and trucks were the most capable and reliable in various terrains and what kinds of support equipment and systems they needed to travel such vast distances.

The Tank Corps, which Ike was still part of, was invited to send two observers along on the road trip. Ike's heart quickened as he read the memo. This was a real adventure where he would see a huge swath of the American landscape while camping, fishing, and sitting around a campfire at night telling stories. Without hesitation, he put his name forward for consideration to be part of the convoy. Ike also persuaded his friend, Major Sereno Brett, to do the same.

On July 8, 1919, amid great fanfare, the 1919 Motor Transport Corps Convoy, as it was officially called, set out for San Francisco from the White House in Washington, DC. Ike and Sereno received their orders to be part of the event at the last moment and so joined the convoy when it stopped at Frederick, Maryland, for the first night.

Ike watched as the convoy reached Frederick. It was quite a sight as eighty-one army vehicles rolled, lurched, and rattled down the main street of town. The convoy included all makes of American trucks, cars, and vans, along with an ambulance, a water truck, two gasoline trucks, twelve motorcycles, two motorized kitchens, two rolling machine shops, a tractor, and even a Renault tank tied down on a flatbed trailer. The crowd cheered and waved flags as the convoy passed. Ike knew that many of the older citizens of Frederick could never have imagined seeing such a sight.

That night Ike and Sereno joined the other members of the convoy at their camp. As they sat around the fire, Ike asked how the first day of travel from Washington had gone. He learned that a number of holdups had occurred along the way, including a two-hour delay because some of the taller vehicles could not fit under a covered wooden bridge and had to ford the river. Also, a truck needed new brakes fitted, a ten-ton rolling machine shop got stuck in mud and caused the convoy to make a detour, a failed magneto on one truck necessitated its being towed, and the Mack trucks struggled with climbing hills even when in first gear—not to mention the other rolling machine shop damaging its roof on another low bridge. As he listened to the tales of woe, Ike wondered what he'd gotten himself into. This was only day one, and they were still east of the Mississippi River, across which the roads were in far worse condition.

The following morning the convoy set out from Frederick for Gettysburg, where they stopped for lunch. From then on they followed the Lincoln Highway. Two scouts on Harley-Davidson motorcycles were sent ahead to survey the roads and measure the height of bridges. Ike thought this was a great idea, since it gave the officers an idea of how to prepare for what lay ahead.

The road the convoy took through Maryland and into Pennsylvania was concrete, though it had originally been built for horses and buggies and was narrow for the ten-ton trucks. As they moved along, Ike realized many of the enlisted men who said they were experienced drivers had exaggerated. Some of them didn't seem to know what a clutch was until they had managed to burn it out. Ike was grateful they wouldn't reach the high mountain passes until later in their trip, since some of the drivers had difficulty just keeping their vehicles on the road. He even overheard one driver yelling "giddy-up" as his truck lost power.

At every stop the convoy made, crowds of people came out to greet them. Local women's groups or the Red Cross provided coffee or lemonade for them, and mayors gave grand speeches.

Once the convoy passed through Chicago, they left behind concrete or macadam-topped roads. As they ventured onto dirt roads, billows of dust made it nearly impossible for drivers at the back of the convoy to see. To combat this, the trucks were spaced out to allow the dust to settle between them. They crossed the Mississippi River at Clinton, Iowa, allowing only a few vehicles on the bridge at a time for fear of it collapsing.

After crossing the Mississippi, they headed across Iowa and then Nebraska before climbing into the high desert of Wyoming, where they crossed the Continental Divide. In Wyoming the towns were spread wide apart, and the vehicles in the convoy had to be refueled from two gasoline trucks. The water supply they carried with them was closely monitored, as the nearest water source was sometimes twenty miles away.

From Wyoming they dropped down into Utah and passed through Salt Lake City before heading out across the Great Basin Desert, which encompassed half of Utah and most of Nevada. The final leg of their long journey would take them into California, over the Sierra Nevada, and then on to the

Pacific Ocean. At the California state line, William Stephens, the state's governor, met the convoy with fanfare and speeches.

On September 6, 1919, sixty days after setting out from Washington, DC, the 1919 Motor Transport Corps Convoy reached its destination—San Francisco. They had driven over 3,200 miles, had 230 road incidents and accidents, and had abandoned nine vehicles along the way. Twenty-one men had left the convoy because of accidents or sickness. Overall, the vehicles that made it had averaged a speed of less than six miles per hour, but to Ike's delight, they had arrived.

In San Francisco the men of the convoy were given new uniforms to wear for a parade along Market Street. A group of mounted police officers led the way, while low-flying army and navy airplanes dropped flowers as the crowd cheered. It was a fitting end to a journey that had passed through 350 communities across the United States and been seen by over three million people.

As the parade made its way along Market Street, Ike felt jubilant, not so much at the convoy's trip being over but because the two-month journey had renewed his enthusiasm for being in the army. He loved the camaraderie, the lasting friendships, the push to know more and do better. And although he had missed out on going to war in Europe, he now understood that he would be an army man for life.

When the celebrations for the end of the 1919 Motor Transport Corps Convoy were over, Ike rode the train east as far as Denver, where he was met at the station by Mamie and Ikky. He had a month's leave, and after a few days relaxing, Ike, Mamie, Ikky, Mamie's parents, and her only remaining sister, Mike (Mable), all drove down to San Antonio in the Douds' touring car. After the trip with the cross-country convoy, Ike felt particularly well equipped to take care of any car problems that might occur along the way.

Before Ike knew it, his leave was over. It was time to return to Camp Meade, where he looked forward to regaling his fellow soldiers with stories of his adventures as part of the convoy. Mamie and Ikky stayed in San Antonio, as there was a housing shortage at Camp Meade following the return of so many soldiers from Europe.

Soon after returning to his duties at Camp Meade, Ike was made commander of the 305th Tank Brigade. Captain George S. Patton, who had graduated from West Point seven years before Ike, was in command of the 304th Tank Brigade, also stationed at Camp Meade. Ike and George became instant friends and spent hours together discussing speed-oriented offensive tank warfare. Both men were convinced that tank warfare would be key to winning wars in the future. George had already served in the 1916 Pancho Villa expedition along the Mexican border and in France, where, as commander of the US Army tank school, he led tanks into combat and was wounded near the end of the war. The two men loved to play poker and ride horses together, during which time they found endless topics of interest to talk about. With their backgrounds in tank warfare they were both particularly interested in reviewing battles to see what difference tanks could have made on the outcome. Every scenario they ran made them both more convinced than ever that tanks would play an important role in future conflicts.

Ike and George's superiors didn't appreciate either man talking so publicly about such radical new warfare ideas. As far as they were concerned, tanks should play only a minor role as a backup for the infantry in any future battles. Ike and George were sure their superiors were mistaken and pressed forward with their ideas, with each man going as far as to write an article for the *Infantry Journal*. Soon after the publication of Ike's article, he was summoned to Washington, DC, to meet with General Charles Farnsworth, chief of the infantry. The general threatened to court-martial Ike if he did not stop talking and writing about his far-fetched ideas on tank warfare. After his dressing down in Washington, Ike continued to meet privately with George about new strategies and possibilities for tank warfare.

Ike had been at Camp Meade about six months when the camp commander decided to allow married officers to set up family homes in the dilapidated war barracks. Mamie and Ikky soon joined him at Camp Meade, and together Ike and Mamie installed a kitchen, a bathroom, and room partitions in the barracks to make an acceptable home for themselves. At last Ike, Mamie, and Ikky were all living together again.

The new married quarters worked out perfectly, as the young family's next-door neighbors were

Beatrice and George Patton and their two daughters, Bea and Ruth Ellen. Bea was old enough to watch Ikky, and together the three children had wonderful adventures fishing for tadpoles in the nearby ditches. Everyone at Camp Meade seemed to love Ikky, and Ike loved to take him to watch football practice, tank maneuvers, and parades. All of it fascinated Ikky. Before long the soldiers of the 305th Tank Brigade pooled their money and had a tiny tanker uniform made for Ikky and taught him how to snap to a smart salute when he was wearing it. They also made him the brigade mascot. Ike and Ikky loved every minute of it.

Soon after Ike and his family had settled into their new accommodations, George invited Ike and Mamie for Sunday lunch. George had a special guest he wanted them to meet. That guest turned out to be Brigadier General Fox Conner. Ike was already well aware of who Fox Conner was. The general had served as operations officer for the American Expeditionary Force during the war in Europe and had won praise for his work in that position. The brigadier general spoke quietly with a southern drawl, and Ike liked him immediately. Soon Ike, George Patton, and General Conner were deep in conversation about the new role tanks could play in the military. Fox Conner wanted to know more about tanks, so Ike and George offered him a full tour of their tank brigades. After lunch the three men spent several hours huddled in conversation.

As Christmas 1920 drew near, Mamie did everything she could to make it a special time when they would all be together as a family. A bright red tricycle sat under the Christmas tree, and a variety of traditional German and Swedish cakes and candies were set out on the sideboard. Two days before Christmas, Ike and Mamie became alarmed—Ikky was feverish. They called the doctor right away, and he told them Ikky had probably eaten something that didn't agree with him and would feel better soon. But the next morning his fever was worse, and Ike and Mamie took him to the camp hospital.

Over the next few days, Ikky's temperature rose and fell, but no one seemed to know what the problem was. Eventually Ike called in a specialist from Johns Hopkins Hospital in Baltimore. After checking Ikky over, the doctor diagnosed his condition as scarlet fever. Ike's heart sank. As with so many childhood illnesses, there was no cure for scarlet fever: a child either recovered or died. To make matters worse, Mamie had come down with a bad cold that looked like it was turning into pneumonia and was bedridden at home. There was no cure for her illness either, and Ike spent his time alternating between the camp hospital and his wife's bedside, willing them both to get well. On the morning of January 2, 1921, Ike sat in the hospital holding Ikky when he stopped breathing. His three-year-old son had just died in his arms. Ike could barely process what had happened. He knew he now had to go home and break the terrible news to Mamie, who was making a slow recovery from her illness.

Soldiers from the tank brigade formed an honor guard as Ikky's small coffin was carried to the train station. There they gently lifted the coffin into a luggage car. Wearily, Ike and Mamie boarded the train that would carry them and the body of their son to Denver, where he would be buried beside Mamie's two sisters. Ike felt like he was in a nightmare from which he would never awake.

Chapter 9

Canal Zone

On January 7, 1922, a year and five days after the death of their son, Ike and Mamie stood on the deck of the *San Miguel*, an army transport ship bound for Panama. It had been a tough twelve months for both of them. They missed Ikky terribly, and Ike knew they were both too heartbroken to properly care for each other as they dealt with their own grief. Ike hoped his new posting to the US Canal Zone in Panama would give them a fresh perspective and a new start.

After departing New York City, the ship steamed down the eastern coast of the United States. Ike liked to stand on deck and scan the horizon for possible storms. He hoped they wouldn't encounter any on this trip. Shortly before departure, Mamie had learned she was pregnant again. Ike was grateful that as the senior officer traveling, he was allocated a spacious cabin with a private bathroom. But at the last moment a general decided to hitch a ride to Panama on the ship, forcing Ike and Mamie to give up their spacious cabin for him. Instead they spent the five days of the voyage packed into a cabin with barely enough room for two bunks and a chair. Ike knew that Mamie was distressed about the trip south, but Mamie also fretted about what they would find upon arrival in Panama.

In many ways, Ike realized he'd married his opposite. Mamie loved clothes and fashion, planning popular dinner parties, and reading romance novels. She was not cut out for a rugged life, as he was. She would never choose to go camping, play a sport, or take a long hike. But Ike was grateful that Mamie had insisted on coming with him to this new posting, even though she was concerned about giving birth to the new baby due in August.

Ike also thought about his new posting. In late 1921, General Fox Conner had taken command of an infantry brigade in Panama and specifically requested that Ike be posted to Panama to serve as his executive officer. The infantry brigade was part of the Panama Canal Department created in 1917 as a separate command of the US Army. After the 1914 completion of the Panama Canal, connecting the Atlantic and Pacific Oceans across the Panamanian isthmus, the Panama Canal Department was created to police and defend the US-controlled Canal Zone. The Canal Zone consisted of not just the canal but also a large swath of land on both sides of it. Ike was honored that Fox Conner had requested him and believed that he could learn a lot from the general.

The voyage to Panama was worse than Ike had anticipated. Off Cape Hatteras the *San Miguel* encountered a violent storm that caused the vessel to pitch and roll, making it too dangerous for Ike and Mamie to leave their cabin. Mamie became extremely seasick and sat propped up in the chair until the storm quieted. In fact, she was too claustrophobic to climb into her bunk and spent every night of the voyage curled up in the chair. After making stops in Puerto Rico and Port-au-Prince, Haiti, the ship docked on the Atlantic side of Panama. After disembarking, Ike and Mamie were both grateful to be on dry land again, but their ordeal wasn't yet over.

An aide to General Fox Conner was waiting at the dock for Ike and Mamie. He welcomed them to Panama and arranged for their luggage to be sent to Camp Gaillard, where they were to be stationed. With the luggage arrangements made, Ike, Mamie, and the aide climbed aboard the train that crossed the isthmus of Panama. The train tracks followed the canal closely, and as the train rolled along, Ike could see through the window the muddy water of the Panama Canal. He was impressed by the verdant jungle visible in almost every direction.

When the train stopped in what appeared to Ike to be the middle of nowhere, the aide informed him and Mamie that this was where they needed to leave the train to reach Camp Gaillard. Once off the train, a catwalk barely wide enough for a car connected their stop to the camp. Mamie hesitated, and Ike had to encourage her every step of the way across. She held his arm with one hand and the single rope handrail with the other. Once safely on the other side, they walked up a muddy track into Camp Gaillard.

Most of Camp Gaillard's buildings had been erected by the French nearly forty years before in their failed attempt to build the Panama Canal. The camp houses were perched precariously on a hill-side above the Culebra Cut, the massive eight-mile-long valley dug through the mountains that formed Panama's Continental Divide and through which the canal now flowed as it connected two oceans.

When Ike and Mamie first saw the house assigned them, Ike took a deep breath. He half expected his wife to turn around and get right back on the train. The place was a disaster by anyone's standards. It was a large two-story structure situated on stilts with verandas on all four sides. In places the deck of the veranda had rotted through, and Ike and Mamie had to tread carefully. There was also no glass in any of the windows. Instead a lattice of wooden strips was nailed across each window opening which was then covered with close mesh wire netting to keep out bugs. It was obvious the house hadn't been occupied in a while. Vines clung to the wire netting, and inside, mold and mildew were everywhere. The place also seemed infested with cockroaches, spiders, lizards, and snakes. As well, Ike could see rusted holes in the iron roof. However, Mamie did not turn and run. Together she and Ike moved into their assigned house and agreed to work together on cleaning up and improving the place.

The following evening, Ike and Mamie were invited to dinner at the Conners' house next door. After pushing through the large hibiscus hedge that separated the two houses, Ike and Mamie felt they had entered another world. While the Conners' house was also an old French-built affair on stilts, it was absolutely immaculate, surrounded by a beautiful garden and neat new rocking chairs on the veranda. Inside everything was clean, freshly painted, and tastefully decorated. As Virginia Conner showed them around her house, she explained it had been in the same condition as Ike and Mamie's when she and her husband arrived at Camp Gaillard. With a little money and some effort, the Conners were able to transform the place inside and out. It also helped that Virginia Conner's father was a millionaire, who provided the money and lavish new furniture for the transformation.

While Ike was impressed with the way the Conners had renovated their home—making mental notes of ways he could improve their own house as he went—he was mostly in awe of General Conner's well-stocked library. He ran his fingertips along the spines of the books arranged neatly on shelves and noticed how the general's eyes lit up when Ike asked him about his book collection. Many of the books were related to military strategy and military history, and there were biographies of famous soldiers and a number of volumes on philosophy. As they talked, General Conner offered to lend Ike as many of the books as he would like and to teach him all he knew about those subjects. It was a great honor for Ike to have the general offer to mentor him, and he gratefully accepted. He was glad he did, because he soon discovered he had plenty of time to read and study.

Each week Monday through Friday, Ike rode horseback alongside Fox Conner as they carried out reconnaissance missions to make sure everything was running as it should throughout their area of the Canal Zone. This meant they were often away all day and sometimes camped out in the jungle overnight. For Ike this was the kind of adventure he'd dreamed of since he was a boy, even if the horse riding sometimes aggravated the pain he felt in his injured knee.

But while he loved the adventure of being out in the jungle, Ike knew that Mamie was struggling. She complained of barely sleeping because howler monkeys howled across the jungle to each other from the tops of trees all night long. They sounded like packs of wild dogs. She heard lots of other strange noises, including a rat who spent the first night in the house gnawing on a chair leg in their bedroom. Bats were everywhere too, and Mamie hated bats. Sometimes at night they squeezed under the door and dive-bombed their mosquito nets. When this happened, Ike knew there would be no more sleep for him until he got up and killed the offending bat with whatever implement he had on hand. Since their early days of marriage, Mamie had prided herself on being a meticulous homemaker. But here she lost hope of ever winning the never-ending battle of stopping mold and mildew growing overnight on anything made of cotton or leather.

Nonetheless, Ike had faith that his wife would adjust to life on the edge of the jungle. Virginia Conner showed Mamie how to place the four bed legs in cans filled with kerosene to stop the march of ants climbing up them. Mamie also learned to take the bedframe outside once a week and cover the springs with newspaper, which she then set alight to heat up the iron frame and kill any bedbugs hiding on it. Then she would fumigate the mattress and bedclothes, and when everything was properly aired out, she would return it all to the bedroom. Ike knew Mamie wouldn't enjoy doing such things at the best of times, but being pregnant made the work all the harder.

The Eisenhowers had been living in the Canal Zone for three months when Mamie's parents and sister Mike came to visit. They were shocked at the primitive conditions the two of them lived under. Mamie's plan was to give birth to the new baby at Camp Gaillard's medical clinic. However, her parents had other ideas. They decided that Mamie would return with them to Denver to give birth.

Mamie, her sister, and their parents departed on April 20, 1922, to sail back to the United States, leaving Ike with more time than ever to read and study. By now, he was busily following Fox Conner's reading recommendations. Fox started Ike out reading several novels based on military themes in Europe, especially during the Napoleonic period. Then he moved on to the memoirs of Civil War generals

Ulysses S. Grant and William Tecumseh Sherman. After Ike finished each book, General Conner questioned him about his understanding of what he'd just read. From Civil War generals they moved onto philosophical works by Plato and Cicero, followed by Carl von Clausewitz's *On War.*

Some of the books were challenging reads, and Ike sometimes had to reread sections of them two or three times to understand their meaning. In the case of *On War,* he had to read the whole book twice. However, with General Conner's constant encouragement and prodding, Ike persisted in his reading and study. While the two men were horseback riding, Ike liked nothing better than to discuss and explore with the general the meaning of some chapter he'd read the night before. With each discussion Ike realized his knowledge of warfare was growing.

Ike had arranged for some leave in late July, hoping to make it to Denver before the birth of the new baby. He made it there in time, and on August 3, 1922, Mamie gave birth to another son. He looked just like Ikky, with wisps of blond hair and bright blue eyes. They named him John Sheldon Doud Eisenhower, after Mamie's father. Ike was able to stay with his wife and new son until the end of the month, when he returned alone to the Canal Zone. Mamie promised to follow him back to Panama as soon as John was old enough to travel.

By October 1922, everything in Ike's world was going well. Mamie and baby John were back with Ike at Camp Gaillard, arriving just in time to learn he'd been awarded the Distinguished Service Medal for his "exceptionally meritorious and distinguished services to the Government of the United States" commanding the Tank Corps Training Center at Camp Colt. The medal citation praised Ike for his display of "unusual zeal, foresight, and marked administrative ability in the organization, training, and preparation for overseas service of technical troops of the Tank Corps." Ike was proud of his Distinguished Service Medal. He was the only member of his West Point class to be awarded the medal, even though most of his fellow classmen had fought overseas.

As Ike continued to read and study, General Conner impressed on him many ideas. But the point the general was most clear about and emphasized repeatedly was his firm belief that a second great war would occur before Ike ever retired from the army. In General Conner's opinion, the Germans had been humiliated by the victorious Allies in the post-war treaties they'd been forced to sign. As a result, he believed a time was coming when the Germans would rise up to reclaim the land they felt was taken from them unfairly. Ike had no difficulty believing this. He and George Patton had tossed around the same idea during their talks together back at Camp Meade. But Fox Conner took things a step further. He told Ike he believed the only way the Allies could win the second war was if they united under one command. He also noted that this would be nearly impossible to accomplish, since each Allied country had its own style of leadership and military pride. Over and over again, General Conner told Ike he felt that only one man was capable of assuming control of all Allied forces, and that was Major George C. Marshall.

Two and a half years in Panama passed quickly for Ike. Before he knew it, General Conner was off to a new assignment in Washington, DC, to serve as deputy chief of staff for the US Army. Ike waited patiently, knowing that he too would soon be assigned to a new posting.

In September 1924, Ike was disappointed to learn he'd been posted back to Camp Meade. He'd hoped he would be accepted into the Infantry School at Fort Benning, Georgia, since that was the next step for an officer wanting to make his mark in the army. The school didn't accept any officer over thirty-six years of age, and Ike would turn thirty-four the following month. Time was slipping away for him.

Camp Meade held terrible memories of Ikky's death, and neither Ike nor Mamie was eager to return there, but orders were orders, and the couple departed Panama with two-year-old John in tow.

Within weeks of arriving, Ike felt as though he'd never left Camp Meade, except for one thing: his good friend George Patton had moved on. While Ike was in Panama, George had attended the Command and General Staff College, graduating twenty-fifth out of 248 students. With that advanced training under his belt, he was now serving as an assistant chief of staff in Boston, Massachusetts.

Ike couldn't help but compare his lack of progress in the army to George Patton's success. He needed to get more training before he was too old. The regular path for a career infantryman was to attend the Infantry School in Georgia and, after successfully completing that school, be sent on to the Command and General Staff College. From there an officer would be assigned to a command post where he could prove himself once more. If his superiors thought he had the potential to be a top leader in the army, he would be sent to the War College in Washington, DC.

Ike decided to take matters into his own hands. He went to the War Office in Washington to plead his case for going to the Infantry School at Fort Benning. The answer he received in Washington was no, he should stay at Camp Meade where he had been assigned. But within days of his visit to the War Department, Ike received a puzzling telegram from General Conner that read, "No matter what orders you receive from the War Department, make no protest. Accept them without question."

Within days Ike was shocked to learn he was being assigned to Fort Logan in Denver, Colorado, to be a recruiting officer. This posting wasn't even under the infantry but was under the Adjunct General Corps and was considered a dead-end assignment. Under normal circumstances Ike would have marched right back to Washington and demanded an explanation, but he was sure Fox Conner was pulling strings somewhere up the chain of command. Because of this, he accepted the new post, and he and Mamie moved yet again.

Fort Logan had its advantages. It was close to Mamie's parents, who loved to help take care of John. Ike was happy for Mamie, especially in light of the difficult time she'd endured in Panama. Ike liked the change of pace too. He kept regular hours and could complete his duties without much effort, leaving him plenty of time to continue studying war tactics. He hoped that somehow he'd soon make it to the Infantry School at Fort Benning.

Chapter 10

Preparing in Peace for War

On Monday, September 7, 1925, the Command and General Staff School at Fort Leavenworth, Kansas, opened with 248 students enrolled. One of them was Dwight Eisenhower. Two months earlier Ike had been surprised to learn that General Conner had used his connections to get Ike into this school without his first having to attend the Infantry School at Fort Benning. This was a big step, and Ike was concerned that he wouldn't be as prepared as the other students, but General Conner wrote him a letter reassuring him he would do well. "You may not know it, but because of your three years' work in Panama, you are far better trained and ready for Leavenworth than anybody I know." Even so, Ike knew the yearlong school would take every ounce of his concentration.

Upon arrival at Fort Leavenworth, Ike was grateful to learn that because of his rank, he and Mamie had been assigned the best family student housing at the fort. The spacious four-room apartment came with central heat and a gas stove. There was plenty of living space for the three Eisenhowers, while Ike used one of the top-floor rooms as his study. The apartment was located in Otis Hall, which was far quieter than the much larger Beehive across the street where most of the Command and General Staff School students and their families were housed in smaller, noisier quarters. As they moved into their new apartment and unpacked, Ike soon saw some familiar faces—those of students from his West Point graduating class who were attending the school and that of Leonard "Gee" Gerow, a buddy from Fort Sam Houston in San Antonio. Although Ike and Gee hadn't seen each other in eight years, they were soon bantering as they used to at Fort Sam.

While Mamie took charge of arranging everything in the apartment, Ike attended the school's orientation classes. The first decision students were asked to make was how they wanted to study. They were given three choices: form a group of up to eight men and study together, choose one study partner, or study alone. Ike ran through the options in his head. A group of up to eight people meant a lot of small talk among them and difficulty making sure everyone in the group pulled his weight. Studying alone, though, could get tedious, especially when it came to working through battle simulations. Ike concluded the best plan for him was to work with a partner, someone as hardworking and quick thinking as he was. Right away Gee Gerow came to mind.

When Ike approached Gee about the possibility of the two of them being study partners, he exclaimed he'd had the same idea. Ike and Gee set up their "command study center" in Ike's top-floor room. They pinned large maps to the walls and scattered paper and pencils on a large table in the center of the room. Although there were a few mandatory classes to attend, most of the coursework at the Command and General Staff School consisted of the students being presented with tactical problems to solve. Each day the students were given a sheet of paper that contained some military problem. Perhaps, for example, blue force was crossing a river when they were attacked en masse by an opposing force. Half of blue force was across the river and the rest were either crossing or waiting to cross. The students were asked to consider the situation and state how they thought blue force should respond.

Students were expected to think through the problem and come up with the best tactical plan to respond to it. Once they had decided this, they wrote it down and handed their paper in. This was followed by a class discussion where the solution "approved" by the school's instructors was laid out and students then worked out all the necessary logistics for moving men and equipment to accomplish the approved solution.

Many of the officers attending the school found this kind of study draining, but the approach invigorated Ike. He'd loved the thrill of solving complex battle plans ever since he and George Patton had gotten into the habit of recreating them back at Camp Meade. In fact, George, who had recently completed the same school, sent Ike a copy of all his class notes. And while the tactical problems they were given to solve weren't all exactly the same, Ike had worked through many of them from George's notes in preparation for the school.

The officers attending the school were also expected to do practical exercises on horseback, riding for hours at a time along limestone bluffs or on the marshy river bottomland. Many officers complained about this, but Ike found it routine. After all, he'd spent three years in Panama riding through the jungle on horseback five days a week. Thankfully, his bad knee held up well.

As the year went on, the pace of learning got faster and the pressure ramped up. Each student had to prove to the army that he was capable of making sound decisions while under pressure.

During weekends Ike and Gee took time off to relax. They had both learned to play golf at Leavenworth's new golf course, and although Ike hardly ever won a round, he fell in love with the game. Ike was grateful that Mamie had become friends with Gee's wife, Katie, who had been a military nurse in Europe during the war. The two women spent a lot of time together since their husbands were so busy.

As his year of studying in the Command and General Staff School sped by, Ike was happier than ever. He'd found his niche in the army making war plans and outlining the thousands of details that needed to be implemented to carry them out. At the end of the school, he was delighted to learn that he'd finished top in his class. General Conner had been right all along: Ike's three years in Panama had given him the skills and mindset he needed to succeed at the Command and General Staff School. Now Ike eagerly awaited his next appointment. Soon he learned he was being sent to Fort Benning, where he was to be given a battalion to lead. He was happy enough with the post, knowing that most career men in the army alternated administrative postings with those of active leadership.

Before departing to take up his new duties, Ike was due some leave. Abilene, Kansas, was only about 130 miles from Fort Leavenworth, and Ike used his leave for something new—a family reunion. Since leaving Abilene to attend West Point fifteen years before, Ike had never been with his five brothers in the same place. They were all scattered across the United States from Washington State to Washington, DC, but each brother was taking the time and making the effort to return to his roots. As a child, Ike had never imagined them all moving away from their family home, marrying, having children, and leading lives of their own. And now they were all headed back to Abilene for three days with one another and their aging parents.

Somehow all six Eisenhower brothers squashed themselves into the same small house where they had spent most of their childhood. Ida Eisenhower cooked her sons their favorite family recipes while the "boys" spent hours comparing the different paths their lives had taken. Arthur, who had left home to be a bank messenger boy, was now a prominent bank manager in Kansas City. Edgar was still living in Tacoma, Washington, and doing well as an attorney. Roy had put himself through pharmacy school and owned a pharmacy in Junction City, Kansas. Earl was an electrical engineer in Pennsylvania, and Milton had risen to become the assistant to the Secretary of Agriculture in Washington, DC. While his mother didn't easily say so, Ike knew that inside she beamed with pride at what each of her sons had accomplished.

Ike's father, David, was now sixty-three years old and still managing the local gas plant. As usual, he said as little as he had to, but Ike was sure it meant a lot to him to have his six sons home together.

On the last morning of their reunion, the Eisenhower brothers took a walk down Abilene's Buckeye Avenue. As they passed the courthouse and crossed the railroad tracks, they linked arms and marched down the middle of the street. Ike smiled as he walked, thinking, *These Eisenhower boys might have started out on the south-side. But look, they've each made something of themselves.*

Ike's time at Fort Benning was very short. By November he'd received orders to go to Washington, DC, where General John Pershing had personally requested him. Ike was about to become a writer. General Pershing had been named to head up a new department: the American Battle Monuments Commission. Ike's job would be to write a guidebook to the places where American forces had fought in

1917–1918, during what was now being referred to as the Great War. The job would also entail making recommendations about what kind of memorial marker should be placed at each site. Ike thought it ironic that he'd been requested for the job, since he was one of the few officers he knew who hadn't set foot in Europe during the war. Still, he had a lot of report-writing experience and was confident he could do a good job.

Ike and Mamie moved to Washington, DC, in January 1927. Mamie had been ill with stomach problems, and she and Ike were relieved they would be near Walter Reed Hospital. Mamie had already spent time there trying to get a correct diagnosis of her illness.

Finding a new place to live was their first challenge upon arrival in Washington. Mamie trudged around the city in the snow, looking for a possible home for them. In the end they settled on an elegant eight-story apartment building called the Wyoming, where Gee Gerow and his wife, Katie, were already living. Ike and Mamie rented a two-bedroom apartment on the fourth floor and moved in.

It was amazing how quickly everyone settled into their new routine. Four-year-old John loved to sit at the window and watch the cars, trolleys, bicycles, and even the occasional horse and buggy roll up and down nearby Columbia Road. Mamie cooked and cleaned, shopped at the commissary at Greenleaf Park with her friends, and planned dinner parties and other social events. Meanwhile, Ike was able to walk to his new job.

General Pershing had served as commander of the American Expeditionary Forces (AEF) on the Western Front in France during the Great War. Afterward Congress created and honored him with the new rank of general of the Armies of the United States, the highest rank in the US Armed Forces. General Pershing was thirty years older than Ike and had been a part of many US battles, starting with the Indian campaigns in New Mexico territory in 1886. Ike learned that Pershing's wife and three of his four children had died in a house fire before the war, which helped him understand why the general seemed so distant and difficult to get to know.

One thing Ike hadn't counted on with the move to Washington was how much he would like living near his youngest brother, Milton. They were nine years apart in age, and Milton had been only eleven when Ike left for West Point. As a result, the two brothers hadn't known each other well. Now, as adults, Ike realized that he and Milton were probably the most alike of all the brothers. The two soon learned to trust each other and spent hours discussing both personal and professional issues. As the assistant to the Secretary of Agriculture, Milton moved in the rarefied upper circles of Washington society. He was often a guest of President Coolidge at the White House and other high-level social events. The two brothers became inseparable, with Ike often accompanying Milton to these parties. Nearly everywhere he went, Ike was referred to as Milton's brother. When Milton and his fiancée, Helen, were married, Ike was his brother's best man. Helen and Mamie got along well too, and the four of them spent many happy hours playing bridge together.

Once again, Ike, Mamie, and John had barely settled in when their lives were turned upside down. This time Ike was offered a place studying at the Army War College. The good news was the college was located at Greenleaf Point in Washington, DC, which meant that the family didn't have to move again.

Classes at the Army War College began August 27, 1927 and would run until June 30, 1928. For Ike, the approach was completely different from the Command and General Staff School. The pressure-filled school at Fort Leavenworth was designed to train army staff officers how to think and react quickly and effectively under stress. The purpose of the Army War College was to train men who were potential generals in the overall art and understanding of warfare. Classes focused on the bigger picture of how armies were organized, mobilized, and deployed. The school also taught about how to prepare for future wars.

As part of their study, each student had to research and write a paper on a subject relevant to the military. Ike researched and wrote a paper titled "An Enlisted Reserve for the Regular Army." In the paper he highlighted the need for the army to increase its supply of reserve forces in case of the outbreak of another war, despite the nation's overall isolationist stance. Public interest in fighting and military spending were at an all-time low. Most people in the United States believed that the nation, along with the Allies, had already fought and won the Great War. As far as they were concerned there would never be another war like that. However, Ike was not one of those people, and he laid out a step-by-step plan to develop and grow an army reserve in readiness for when the next full-scale war erupted. He pointed out that for a nation unwilling to spend much money on its armed forces, having a reserve of men to draw on was much less expensive than employing such men on an ongoing basis as regular soldiers.

After completing his studies at the Army War College, Ike was given a choice for his next position. He could either accept a post at the War Department as general staff or return to the American Battle Monuments Commission and revise the guidebook he had written. This posting involved moving to Paris for a year to gather information firsthand.

Ike was eager to take up the position with the War Department, which he saw as a step toward promotion. However, Mamie really wanted to go to Paris. Ike knew that his wife dreamed of traveling and that their only overseas post to the Panama Canal Zone had been difficult for her. Ike also thought of the other sacrifices Mamie had made for his career and so reluctantly opted to return to the American Battle Monuments Commission and the posting to Paris.

On July 31, 1928, Ike, Mamie, and John, along with Mamie's parents, set sail from New York City for France. John was excited as they set out. His sixth birthday was just three days away. Ike tried to be excited too, for himself and for his son, but all he could think was that he was sidelining his career. And for what? To trudge around overgrown battlefields in France and Belgium, recording other officers' wartime exploits.

Chapter 11

Glorified Desk Jobs

Upon arrival in Paris, the Eisenhowers rented a second-floor apartment a mile from the Eiffel Tower on the left bank of the Seine River. Because American dollars went a long way in postwar Paris, their fully furnished four-bedroom living quarters were more luxurious than anything they could have afforded in the United States. They even had enough money in their budget to pay two servants to take care of the housework.

Paris was a dazzling, fast-paced city, and whenever Ike and Mamie could, they went to jazz clubs to dance and socialize. Their apartment also became a hub for army friends and overseas visitors. Ike liked to cook American meals for their guests to remind them of home.

The American Battle Monuments Commission offices were within easy walking distance of the new apartment, and Ike soon found himself engrossed in his work. In the nineteen months the United States had been involved in the Great War, more than two million American soldiers had served in Western Europe. Fifty-two thousand had lost their lives there, and another 203,000 had been wounded. The commission's purpose was to provide clear and complete instructions for anyone wanting to visit the places where American soldiers had died and to plan appropriate memorials at those sites. It was a long and exacting undertaking requiring many trips into the French countryside.

Having enjoyed researching battles from childhood, Ike loved the job. He took French lessons every afternoon and made great progress reading and writing the language, but he struggled to speak it. Fortunately, the American Battle Monuments Commission provided him with a car and chauffeur, who also functioned as Ike's French interpreter.

While stationed at Camp Colt in Gettysburg, Ike had spent many hours hiking the old Civil War battlefields. But the battlefields of France and Belgium were very different. The Great War had ended ten years before, but the land still bore the scars of the intense fighting. Rusting coils of razor wire still stretched across the ground, which was cratered and pockmarked from shell and hand grenade explosions. Lengths of the trenches remained intact, with gooey mud in the bottom. And the hulks of destroyed and abandoned tanks and other equipment dotted the landscape. Ike was surprised to learn that bodies of dead soldiers were still being discovered.

At the end of Ike's yearlong posting to France, he was confident he had a broader understanding of the US Army's strategy and tactics during the Great War than anyone other than perhaps Generals John Pershing and Fox Conner.

In September 1929, the Eisenhowers departed France aboard the *Leviathan* and headed back to the United States. While they were in Paris, Ike and Mamie had sublet the apartment at the Wyoming building for the year and now moved straight back into it. It felt good being back in familiar surroundings. But within a month of their return, the United States was turned upside down.

Over several days at the end of October 1929, the New York Stock Exchange suffered a series of share price drops that caused the stock market to crash. Throughout the 1920s not only banks but also regular Americans had invested heavily in stocks. Some even borrowed money to do so. With the stock market crash, billions of dollars in American wealth were wiped away. The crash spread quickly around the world and pushed the United States into an economic crisis. Banks began to fail and close without returning customers' deposits. People were laid off from their jobs and lost their homes to foreclosure. Before long, many Americans were reduced to sleeping and begging in the streets or lining up at soup kitchens for food.

Ike was relieved that Mamie's parents lost little money in the stock market crash and retained ownership of their homes in Denver and San Antonio. But as he watched the economic depression take hold in the country, he wasn't hopeful about his future in the army. American military spending had already been tight before the crash, and Ike was sure it would be one of the first things the government cut further as it tried to deal with the declining economic situation.

By now Ike had begun his next assignment: serving as executive officer to General George V. Moseley, assistant secretary of war. During the Great War, the United States had been slow to begin producing equipment and weapons. Ike had firsthand knowledge of this from his time leading the Tank Corps at Camp Colt. The war had ended by the time US-produced tanks were ready to ship to France. General Moseley decided that the best way to prepare for another war was to have existing manufacturing plants quickly change focus and produce weapons and equipment. The approach made sense to Ike. A Ford motorcar assembly plant could easily shift to making tanks, or a shoemaking factory to manufacturing waterproof boots and pouches for soldiers. Ike's job as General Moseley's executive officer was to determine which industries could quickly convert to manufacturing war equipment and to ask if factory owners were willing to plan ahead with him.

Once more, this involved a lot of travel and research. While this had its challenges given the economic depression, Ike liked getting out of Washington and into the world of regular people. His biggest challenge was getting factory owners to take him seriously. The Great War was still fresh in people's minds, and people hoped there would never be another one like it. "Wasn't that the war to end all wars?" many factory owners quizzed Ike. They had no desire to spend time and effort planning to convert their facilities into war machines should the United States be drawn into another great war.

Three years rolled by, and on March 4, 1933, Franklin D. Roosevelt was sworn in as the 32nd president of the United States. In the time leading up to the election, he'd campaigned on a platform he called the New Deal, a series of programs, public works projects, financial reforms, and regulations all designed to free the United States from the grip of ongoing economic depression. Around the time President Roosevelt was sworn into office, General Douglas MacArthur, US Army chief of staff, requested that Ike become his chief military aide.

While Ike longed to be leading troops in a hands-on way, he felt entrenched in Washington, DC. He wondered if he had made a mistake taking the American Battle Monuments Commission appointment. Still, he had to admit that staying in Washington had its advantages. Mamie was happy there, and they had many local friends, including Gee Gerow and Ham Haislip. And ten-year-old John was progressing well at John Quincy Adams School, where he was in fifth grade. Ike's brother, Milton, and his wife, Helen, still lived there, along with their two-year-old son, Milton Eisenhower Jr. Milton Sr. had climbed steadily up the political ladder in Washington and was now the director of information for the Department of Agriculture.

President Roosevelt was serious about his New

Deal, but because the money for the programs had to come from somewhere, he slashed military spending by 51 percent. Ike was torn. General MacArthur threatened to resign over the cuts, while Milton now served as the president's spokesman for the New Deal.

Ike was relieved when MacArthur's term as US Army chief of staff ended in October 1935. Ike was convinced that now he could get back to commanding troops. But Douglas MacArthur had other ideas. He called Ike into his office and asked him to go to the Philippines with him as his personal aide. Ike made up excuses, until the general made his request an order. Like it or not, Ike's next post would involve a lot of politics in another big city.

The question became whether Mamie and John should accompany Ike to the Philippines. Mamie still had flashbacks of living in the Panama Canal Zone and wasn't sure she could put herself and her health through living in a second tropical country. John was now in eighth grade and wanted to stay with his friends until the end of the school year. Ike adjusted to the fact he would be living without his family in the Philippines, at least for a while.

It made sense to Ike that General MacArthur was off to the Philippines. He had a long and deep connection to the place. His father, General Arthur MacArthur, was the first military governor of the Philippines at the end of the Spanish-American War. After graduating first in his class at West Point, Douglas MacArthur was posted to Manila in the Philippines. Ironically, it was the same path Ike had chosen for himself as a new West Point graduate. But instead of getting the requested Philippines posting, Ike had been sent to Fort Sam Houston in San Antonio, Texas. Now, twenty years later, he was about to make it to the Philippines at last.

Over the next few weeks, Ike reviewed his assignment. The more he learned, the more complicated it appeared. The Philippines comprised over seven thousand islands that had been subjected to waves of immigration and conquest as far back as recorded history told. In 1521 Portuguese explorer Ferdinand Magellan arrived in the Philippines and claimed the islands for Spain, and in 1565 Spanish colonization began. The Spanish ruled the Philippines until 1898, when the United States defeated Spain and the islands became a US territory. In 1934, Congress passed the Tydings-McDuffie Act, which turned the Philippines into a commonwealth with a directly elected president. The act also laid out a path whereby the commonwealth would become an independent nation on July 4, 1946. During this twelve-year period, the United States would gradually hand over more and more power to the Philippine government.

The United States' pledge to prepare the Philippines for independence was where General MacArthur and Ike came into the picture. The general was charged with developing and equipping what would become the Filipino armed forces. Ike would help make that happen.

On Saturday, October 26, 1935, the SS *President Harding* sailed into Manila Bay, Philippines. It was an interesting twenty-five-day voyage for Ike. General MacArthur had brought along his eighty-three-year-old mother, Pinky, who wasn't well. His sister-in-law, Mary, had also come along on the voyage to nurse Pinky. Before setting out, General MacArthur had instructed Ike to choose an assistant to bring with him to the Philippines. Ike chose Jimmy Ord, a friend ever since his West Point class. Jimmy spoke Spanish, which would give him an advantage, since that was the unifying language of the Philippines. But more than that, Jimmy was someone Ike could count on. He was detail-oriented and hardworking. Jimmy's wife and two teenage children, Jimmy Jr. and Letitia, were also traveling aboard the ship. Sometimes Ike felt sad as he observed Jimmy's family interacting with one another. He wished Mamie and John were with him on this new adventure but knew they had stayed behind for good reasons.

In Manila the MacArthurs, the Ords, and Ike moved into the grand Manila Hotel, which would be their new home for the time being. The hotel was a magnificent, green-tile-roofed, mission-style building with 149 rooms. The MacArthurs occupied the penthouse suite, which came with air conditioning, while Ike and the Ords were given beautiful rooms with high ceilings, fans instead of air conditioning, and patio doors that opened to outdoor garden terraces. From his terrace Ike had a sweeping view across Manila Bay.

On Monday afternoon, Douglas MacArthur announced that the offices of the Philippine defense mission he was heading up would be located at 1 Calle Victoria, a round building atop the old stone wall the Spanish had built in the seventeenth century to protect Manila from attack. Ike and Jimmy had upstairs offices with stunning views of Manila and the bay. With ceiling fans humming above them, the two men went to work.

While US Army soldiers were stationed at various posts around the Philippines, the job General MacArthur and his team had come to accomplish was separate. The army was there to defend the Philippines until it became independent. General MacArthur had come to prepare the country to take over its own defense. The biggest threat they would need to defend themselves against appeared to be the Japanese. At the beginning of the 1930s, Japan had begun expanding its influence rapidly in East Asia. It already controlled Korea, and in 1931 the Japanese military seized control of Manchuria in northeastern China. The following year they invaded more of China. Situated less than five hundred miles south of China's coastline, the Philippines cast a wary eye on Japan.

In their new offices, Ike and Jimmy began outlining the areas they needed to develop—finding fit, local men ready to fight, housing them, equipping them, procuring supplies to feed and clothe them, and acquiring transport to move them from place to place, not to mention finding qualified soldiers to train them. It was a daunting task, one General MacArthur assured them the US government was behind. The new Philippine government had even allocated fifty million pesos, a quarter of its annual budget, to get the job done.

Ike expected problems along the way, and the problems started almost immediately. The Philippine budget was slashed by 50 percent, and the US government stalled on its end of the agreement. Ike wasn't surprised. The government didn't have the resources to field a strong army themselves. In fact, the US Army was at an all-time low point, not having even a single unit ready for combat, and it ranked sixteenth among the world's most powerful armies, behind countries like Finland and Turkey.

Ike and Jimmy worked to stay within the revised budget. They created tables for administrative and tactical organization, developed progress charts showing details of the anticipated Philippine army growth, and produced maps showing the location of each unit they established. They drafted laws prescribing the new army's basic organization and methods for registering and inducting trainees. They also wrote plans for establishing military instruction in public schools, which they hoped would eventually bring young men into the new army.

Their plan called for training six thousand men each year to build up a large civil defense. Initially Ike planned to train the recruits in a few large camps. But because the budget wouldn't stretch that far, he mapped out 125 sites throughout the Philippines to train smaller groups of men. Each camp needed buildings, water, lights, roads, drainage, sewage, equipment, and supplies.

Douglas MacArthur soon tired of hearing about all the details and gave Ike the role of meeting with Philippine President Manuel Quezon once or twice a week at Malacañang Palace to go over the plans with him. The two men got along well, and soon President Quezon provided Ike with his own office at the palace. Ike and the president often spent their lunch hours together playing bridge.

Without Mamie and John around, Christmas 1935 was bleak for Ike. It was made bleaker by the fact that General MacArthur's mother had died earlier in the month. Without his mother around, Douglas MacArthur became moody and depressed. Ike spent Christmas Day with the Ord family, which made him miss his wife and son even more.

Getting the first training camps launched created many headaches for Ike. Filipinos spoke eight different languages, within which were ninety dialects. While the Philippines' two official languages were Tagalog and Spanish, few recruits outside the main island of Luzon spoke either, and twenty percent of the population couldn't read or write. The recruits struggled with using a latrine, washing their hands, sleeping on army cots, and following orders they either didn't understand or saw no point to. Ike wondered what kind of soldiers to expect at the end of their training.

Despite these challenges, General MacArthur promised President Quezon a Philippine air force with 250 light planes and pilots. It seemed an impossible dream to Ike. Taking men who rode carabao in the rice fields and teaching them to fly airplanes seemed unrealistic. Nonetheless, the general ordered Ike to start an air force pilot training program in early 1936. Ike was grateful when the US Army Air Corps offered to loan him two American training pilots to help with the task. Ike also managed to scrounge up several light aircraft, including a Boeing/Stearman PT-13, with which to begin the Philippine air force.

No sooner had pilot training begun than the budget was cut again from twenty-five million pesos to sixteen million, less than a third of the money originally promised. Ike and Jimmy slashed their plans once more, reducing training time down to six months. Ike also had learned they could buy stockpiles of old Enfield rifles left over from the Great War for four dollars each from the US government. He was disheartened when informed he'd have to pay eight dollars per rifle instead. He ordered one hundred thousand of them anyway and wondered how committed the US government was to helping the Philippines become militarily self-sufficient.

In late October 1936, after a year on his own, Ike was delighted when Mamie and John arrived in Manila. He still lived at the Manila Hotel, and Mamie decided they should continue doing so, particularly since Douglas MacArthur had installed his own chefs in the hotel kitchen. He insisted they wash all fruit and vegetables before serving them and boil all the water they used. John was enrolled in a Western-style boarding school in Baguio, the summer capital of the Philippines, where the rich and elite vacationed and sent their children to school. Located in the mountains of Luzon, five thousand feet above sea level, Baguio's climate was cool year-round.

As 1936 drew to a close, General MacArthur became impatient with the plan to slowly build up recruitment and training. He ordered Ike to prepare to train forty thousand men the following year. It didn't seem possible, but Ike had to try: orders were orders.

Meanwhile, in 1937 Japan attacked and took control of major coastal cities in China. Then on December 12, the Japanese attacked an American gunboat on the Yangtze River, sinking it and killing two men and injuring thirty others. The Chinese government and its leader Chiang Kai-shek fled inland to Chungking, while American citizens—soldiers, missionaries, and businesspeople—fled the country, many of them arriving in the Philippines.

On January 30, 1938, Jimmy Ord took off on a flight to Baguio with a Filipino student pilot at the aircraft's controls. Ike had urged him to take one of the American instructors along as a pilot, but Jimmy said he had faith in the trainee. As they neared Baguio, the inexperienced pilot stalled the aircraft, which crashed. Jimmy was severely injured, and hours later he died. Ike was devastated. He'd asked Jimmy to come to the Philippines as his assistant, and now his old friend was dead. The task of informing Jimmy's wife and children of his death fell to Ike. It was one of the most difficult things he'd ever had to do.

With Jimmy gone, any joy Ike felt in trying to complete the impossible job of building a Philippine army vanished. He wanted to return to the United States, especially now that the future war he and General Fox Conner had talked about so often in Panama seemed to be drawing closer. Already in Europe, Germany, under the control of Adolf Hitler and the Nazis, had annexed Austria, and in East Asia, Japanese forces were continuing their drive to take control of as much territory as possible.

On Monday, September 4, 1939, Ike and Mamie visited the Smiths' home in Manila. Howard Smith, a colonel in the Public Health Service in the Philippines, was also a radio enthusiast. As Mamie and Mrs. Smith talked, Ike pulled headphones over his ears while Howard tuned his radio to the British Broadcasting Corporation (BBC) in London. Atmospheric conditions were good, and the station came in loud and clear. It was still September 3 in London as Ike listened to the voice of British Prime Minister Neville Chamberlain declare that following Hitler's invasion of Poland that had begun two days prior, Great Britain was now at war with Germany.

While he believed a new war to be inevitable, Ike was still stunned by the news. Now that the British had declared war, he wondered if or how long the United States would stay out of it. What would President Roosevelt do?

Ike knew that if the United States were to get involved in another great war, he would have to get home quickly. His military record of actual time spent commanding troops was minimal. Despite his best efforts, he kept ending up in what he thought were glorified desk jobs. Unless he commanded a battalion in peacetime, there was no way he would be sent overseas. He could well end up sitting out another war.

After four years serving in the Philippines, Ike felt he'd earned the right to ask General MacArthur to release him to return home. At first the general raised objections, but then he agreed to sign off on Ike's return. President Quezon was more persistent when he learned of Ike's plan to leave the Philippines. He offered him a lucrative contract if he stayed. Ike was flattered but explained that as a soldier he'd given his life to serving his country, and if it was to enter into this new war, he needed to be on hand to serve. Reluctantly President Quezon accepted his explanation.

In early December 1939, the Eisenhower family set sail from Manila for the United States, following a lavish going-away party at Malacañang Palace. As he stood on deck looking back at the beautiful Manila Bay coastline, Ike told himself he'd done the best he could during his time there. Would it prove to be enough? He suspected that Japan would soon take advantage of the turmoil in Europe and invade the Philippines. Although the United States was technically in charge of Philippine security, Ike hoped that the troops he had worked hard to recruit and train would be a deciding factor in defending their homeland, though he had his doubts.

Chapter 12

The Big One

On July 1, 1941, Ike and Mamie drove through the gates of Fort Sam Houston in San Antonio, Texas. Ike couldn't help but think of the first time he passed through those gates in mid-September 1915 as an enthusiastic, single twenty-four-year-old, ready to prove himself. Oddly enough, July 1 was also Ike and Mamie's twenty-fifth wedding anniversary. A year and a half had passed since they'd departed the Philippines. In that time Ike had been commander of the 15th Infantry Regiment at Fort Lewis in Washington State. While there, Congress passed the Selective Training and Service Act, which President Roosevelt signed into law on September 1, 1940. The act set up the first peacetime conscription in the United States, requiring all American men between the ages of twenty-one and thirty-six to register for the draft, the lottery system through which a certain number of the registered men were chosen to serve in the armed services.

By the time Ike arrived at Fort Sam Houston, the number of men serving in the armed services had ballooned to 1.4 million and the military budget had increased to nine billion dollars. Ike loved being in the thick of this new surge in activity and in training the raw recruits at Fort Lewis. However, in June 1941, Lieutenant General Walter Krueger, commander of the Third Army at Fort Sam Houston, had requested that Ike serve as his chief of staff. Once more Ike found himself stationed in San Antonio. His new position came with a promotion to colonel.

As well as being Ike and Mamie's twenty-fifth wedding anniversary, July 1 was also the day their nineteen-year-old son John was to report to the United States Military Academy at West Point to begin his army career. Ike's thoughts drifted to John. He was proud of his son's choice but felt a little sorry for Mamie. Now she would have two men in uniform to be concerned about, especially with the threat of war lurking on the horizon. Ike promised his wife they would visit John together at West Point over Christmas vacation.

Ike was grateful that Mamie was there with him to set up house, because he had to get straight to work. Thankfully, as a colonel, he was now entitled to two personal assistants, one a striker and the other an executive assistant. The job of the striker was to help with anything that needed to be done, from running errands to cleaning the house to make it ready for guests. For this position Ike chose Private Mickey McKeogh, the lively son of Irish immigrants who had been a bellhop at New York City's Plaza Hotel. Ike figured that Mickey was used to responding to all sorts of requests. For his executive assistant he chose Lieutenant Ernest "Tex" Lee, who'd been a Chevrolet car salesman before being drafted. Tex was cheerful and efficient, and Ike thought they would make a strong team.

Upon taking up his new position, Ike immediately began preparing the 240,000 men under General Krueger's command to participate in massive war maneuvers to take place in Louisiana in four weeks. The maneuvers had been nicknamed the "Big One," since they involved nearly half a million men, making it the largest such military exercise ever held in the United States.

The Big One was designed with several goals in mind. It would give newly drafted recruits experience following orders on the battlefield and test officers on how well they could direct men and equipment in a real-world situation. This was important because if or when the United States did enter the war slowly engulfing the world, the military would need leaders who understood the latest technologies and how they could be put to use rather than sticking with antiquated battle techniques used in the Great War. Even though that war had ended only twenty-three years before, so much had changed technologically. Submarines, tanks, and airplanes that played only minor roles in the Great War were now more sophisticated and robust and, in the case of airplanes, had become an indispensable platform for dropping bombs on the enemy. Machine guns were also more efficient, as were radios to keep in contact with soldiers on the battlefield and with ships at sea. And radar could track incoming enemy airplanes above, while sonar could detect submarines below.

Ike began working up to twenty hours a day making preparations for the Big One. The maneuvers would take place in a triangle of land situated between the Sabine River to the west, the Calcasieu River to the east, and the Red River to the north, an area that covered 3,400 square miles of Louisiana.

A week before the maneuvers were to begin, a hurricane struck Louisiana. Rivers burst their banks, flooding much of the chosen area. Ike knew this would make conditions much harder for men and vehicles, but it would also be a great test of how tanks fared in deep mud.

For the Big One, the troops involved were divided into two armies: the Red Army led by General Ben Lear, and the Blue Army led by General Krueger. The maneuvers would comprise two phases. In phase one, the Red Army was instructed to cross the Red River on September 15 and invade the Blue homeland. The Blue Army's job was to intercept the Red Army and force it back across the river. In phase two, the Blue Army was given its own tank division, with Ike's old friend George Patton as one of the two tank division commanders. Their job was to advance upon and seize the city of Shreveport, Louisiana. The Red Army's job was to defend the city with a hundred-mile defensive line to the south. Besides trying out new tanks, the Blue Army got to use parachute troops for the first time in US military history. One hundred twenty-seven paratroopers jumped from transport airplanes and landed in a cotton patch to test how effectively they could get behind enemy lines.

By the end of the September maneuvers, Ike had learned a great deal about what did and did not work. The new C rations the soldiers carried proved adequate, paratroopers were fast and carried the element of surprise, tanks were effective even in deep mud, and deaths were unavoidable. Even without real weapons being fired, twenty-six men died during the Big One. One soldier was struck and killed by lightning, several men drowned crossing a river, and motorcycle wrecks and other motorized vehicle accidents occurred.

When the maneuvers were over, an expected shake-up of officers took place. Forty-two officers and commanders had taken part in the maneuvers, at the end of which thirty-one were asked to retire or step aside from their position. Only eleven officers were kept and promoted. Among them was Ike, who had passed the test and was promoted to brigadier general. Ike and the other officers retained were expected to form the core of the new, modern United States Army.

In early December 1941, Ike was still busy winding up final details for the Big One maneuvers, writing and filing reports and recommendations about all that had been learned. On Sunday morning,

December 7, he went to his office to tackle more of the never-ending paperwork. At noon he decided to return home for a nap, telling Mamie that nothing was important enough that it couldn't wait until he woke up. Ike was wrong. An hour later he became aware of Mamie shaking him awake. She uttered four words—Pearl Harbor, Japanese attack—that ricocheted throughout Ike's mind. Immediately he was wide awake.

Few details were available, but the situation sounded bad. At 7:48 a.m. local time in Hawaii, the Japanese navy had launched a surprise air raid on Pearl Harbor. As a result of the aerial bombing, it sounded to Ike like most of the ships in the US Navy's Pacific Fleet had either been sunk in the harbor or were on fire.

Ike rushed back to his office. Throughout the rest of the day and into the evening, he and many of his fellow officers sat glued to the radio. The Japanese followed up the bombing of Pearl Harbor with attacks on Wake Island, Guam, and Davao in the southern Philippines. Nine hours later they attacked Clark Field, fifty miles northeast of Manila. The news of that attack was grim. Somehow seventeen B-17 bombers had been allowed to remain parked on the ground. Twelve were destroyed in the attack and four more seriously damaged. Thirty-four P-40s were also destroyed on the ground. While Pearl Harbor had been a surprise attack, by the time the Japanese attacked Clark Field Ike thought someone in the Philippines should have prepared for the possibility they would be next. Now 80 men were dead,

150 were wounded, and most of the Far East Air Force planes had been destroyed on the ground.

The next day, December 8, Ike and his men listened to the radio again, this time to hear President Franklin Roosevelt speak to a joint session of the US Congress. Ike listened closely as the president declared,

> Yesterday, December 7th, 1941—a date which will live in infamy—the United States of America was suddenly and deliberately attacked by naval and air forces of the Empire of Japan. . . .
>
> The attack yesterday on the Hawaiian Islands has caused severe damage to American naval and military forces. I regret to tell you that very many American lives have been lost. In addition, American ships have been reported torpedoed on the high seas between San Francisco and Honolulu.
>
> Yesterday the Japanese government also launched an attack against Malaya.
>
> Last night Japanese forces attacked Hong Kong.
>
> Last night Japanese forces attacked Guam.
>
> Last night Japanese forces attacked the Philippine Islands.
>
> Last night the Japanese attacked Wake Island.
>
> And this morning the Japanese attacked Midway Island. . . .
>
> As Commander in Chief of the Army and

> Navy, I have directed that all measures be taken for our defense. But always will our whole nation remember the character of the onslaught against us.
>
> No matter how long it may take us to overcome this premeditated invasion, the American people in their righteous might will win through to absolute victory. . . .
>
> I ask that the Congress declare that since the unprovoked and dastardly attack by Japan on Sunday, December 7, 1941, a state of war has existed between the United States and the Japanese empire.

Following President Roosevelt's speech Ike worked around the clock, preparing for equipment to be sent to the West Coast of the United States in case the Japanese bombed there next.

Three days later, the United States also declared war on Germany and Italy. For better or for worse, the country had been drawn into a global conflict against formidable foes to the west and to the east. It was the moment Ike had been anticipating most of his military career.

On Friday, December 12, Ike received a phone call from Colonel Walter Bedell Smith, the secretary of the War Office General Staff. "The chief says to hop on a plane and get here right away," the colonel growled. "Don't worry about written orders. We'll deal with the paperwork later."

Ike put down the phone and took a deep breath. He was just a few days away from setting out with

Mamie to visit John at West Point. Now he had to rush home, tell Mamie about the change of plans, pack a bag, and hitch a ride on an airplane to Washington, DC, as fast as possible. He wasn't sure why someone at the War Department thought he needed to be in Washington in such a hurry, but he didn't ask questions. Duty called, and he would answer, no matter what it required of him.

It took a day and a half for Ike to reach the War Department offices in the Old Munitions Building on Constitution Avenue in Washington, DC. The airplane he'd been traveling on had been forced to land in Dallas, Texas, because of bad weather, and he had taken the train the rest of the way from there.

Upon arrival at the War Department, Ike was immediately taken to see General George Marshall, the US Army chief of staff, and briefed on the latest information about Japanese military attacks and sightings. When General Marshall was finished, he looked up at Ike and asked, "What should the US military do next? What should be our general course of action?"

Ike sat for a moment. There was so much new information to take in, his head was spinning. "Give me a few hours to think things through and prepare a response," he told the general.

General Marshall nodded. "Get someone to give you a desk, and get going," he said, looking at his watch before turning his attention to a pile of papers.

A few minutes later, Ike was reunited with Gee Gerow, his old friend and study partner at the Command and General Staff School. Gee was now chief of the War Plans Division, and he showed Ike to a desk he could use. Gee confided in Ike that two days before, General Marshall had demoted General Walter Short, the commander at Pearl Harbor, and recalled him to Washington, DC. Major General Herbert Dargue of the Army Air Forces had been sent out to replace him. General Dargue and seven other military officers had departed in a Douglas B-18 Bolo aircraft, which had gone missing somewhere over the Sierra Nevada in California. Search parties had been sent out, but there was no sign of the airplane or the men it carried. It was assumed the plane had crashed, killing everyone aboard. Ike had been summoned to Washington to replace Colonel Charles Bundy, one of the missing men.

Ike felt sober as he sat down to work. War had been declared only six days before, and already the US Army had lost a general and seven senior officers at a time when the country could least afford it.

Ike took several hours to think things through and write a response to General Marshall's question. Bearing in mind the weakness of the Philippine army and the crippling effect of the loss of most of the Pacific naval fleet, Ike couldn't see any way to save the Philippines from being overrun by the Japanese. Yet the eyes of the world were on the United States to see how the country responded to the Japanese attacks on Pearl Harbor and the Philippines. If the United States did nothing, it would look as if it didn't care for its allies. But Ike knew that if they tried to save the Philippines at this stage, American forces would be soundly beaten by Japan. Ike could see no good outcome. Nevertheless he decided that the United States needed to do something for the Philippines, and when that failed, American forces should set up an effective sea and air base in Australia from which to counterattack when the time was right. This would cost a lot of money and be risky, but Ike was sure it was the right thing to do. With a sheath of notes in his hand, Ike returned to General Marshall's office.

"So, what do you think?" the general asked Ike as he motioned for him to sit down.

Ike told General Marshall his thoughts on how the United States should do all it could to help the Philippines, while at the same time realizing they would not succeed. "The people of China, of the Philippines, of the Dutch East Indies will be watching us," he concluded. "We must do all that is humanly possible to save them. They may excuse failure, but they will not excuse being abandoned."

Ike looked into General Marshall's steely blue eyes and then heard him say, "I agree. Do what you can to save them." After a pause he continued. "Eisenhower, the War Department is filled with able men who analyze such problems but always feel compelled to bring them to me for a final solution. I must have assistants who will solve their own problems and tell me later what they've done."

Now that's a man I could work for! Ike thought as he left the general's office.

It was dark by the time a staff car dropped Ike off at his brother Milton's house in Falls Church, Virginia, a half-hour drive from the War Department offices. Milton was still Director of Information for the US Department of Agriculture. He invited Ike to stay with him, Helen, and their two children for as long as he wanted. Although Ike knew he would be working long days going forward, he was heartened to know he could talk with Milton in the evenings when he finished work for the night.

Ike soon discovered that his many army postings over the years now fit together to help him in his current post. His time leading the Tank Corps had opened his eyes to how modern technology could change the way wars were fought and open up new opportunities for victory on the battlefield. His time in Panama had brought him close to General Fox Conner, who taught him the importance of preparing for another global war. And his time serving as General Moseley's executive officer had given him insight into how various industries needed to quickly mobilize and switch to producing military equipment. Through time spent in the Philippines he had learned how to adapt to new geography and people and to understand what their strengths and weaknesses were. The time in the Philippines had also taught him how to work with and gain the confidence of political leaders.

In January 1942, Mamie visited Ike in Washington after spending Christmas with John at West Point. Ike was too busy with his war planning work to take even a single day off, and he had been unable to go with her.

When General Marshall had summoned Ike to Washington from San Antonio, Ike wasn't sure how long he would be away. By now it had become clear it was a permanent move—or as permanent as the army could offer in a time of war. Ike wasn't going back to Fort Sam Houston. Washington, DC, would once again be home. He asked Mamie to return to San Antonio to pack up their house yet again, then join him in Washington. When she returned from Texas, they leased a one-bedroom apartment at the Wardman Tower and moved in with a few items from their home at Fort Sam. Accompanying Mamie from Fort Sam were Ike's two aides, Private Mickey McKeogh and Lieutenant Tex Lee. Ike was glad to have them assist him again.

In February, soon after Ike and Mamie moved into their new apartment, Gee Gerow was promoted to commander of the 29th Infantry Division, and Ike replaced him as chief of the War Plans Division. Ike hated to see Gee go, but he knew his friend was the type of person who liked to run his decisions by the boss before implementing them, while General Marshall needed officers under him at the War Department who weren't afraid to make decisions on their own and carry them out.

As Gee turned his office over to Ike, he commented, "I got Pearl Harbor on the book, lost the Philippine Islands, Singapore, and Sumatra. Let's see what you can do."

Ike was ready for the challenge.

Chapter 13

The Whole Shebang

Ike was right: American and Filipino soldiers fought as hard as they could, but by early March 1942, Japanese forces were in the final stages of taking control of the Philippines. The US Army focus was now on establishing a base in Australia from which to counterattack Japan when the time was right, as Ike had suggested.

Meanwhile, on March 10, as Ike sat in his office at the War Department drafting a message for President Franklin Roosevelt to send to Chinese leader General Chiang Kai-shek, a phone call from Mamie interrupted him. Her voice cracked as she told Ike his father had died. When he hung up the phone, Ike put his head in his hands for a long moment of silence. He knew he couldn't afford the time to go to Abilene for the funeral and help console his mother. He would have to leave that to his brothers. Instead, he asked his striker Mickey McKeogh to send enough red roses and Easter lilies to blanket his father's casket, knowing it was the best he could do given the circumstance.

Two days later, at the appointed time of David Eisenhower's funeral service, Ike closed his office door for thirty minutes. He sat silently thinking about his father's legacy and wrote a eulogy for him which he tucked away in a notebook. When the half hour was up, he unlocked his office door and turned his attention once more to war plans.

In April 1942, Ike was promoted to the rank of major general, and a month later General George C. Marshall appointed him assistant chief of staff. Although he was now a two-star general, Ike felt further removed from the battlefront than ever.

While the Philippines had been overrun by the Japanese in the east, two years earlier in the west, German forces had overrun France. On June 22, 1940, the French government signed an armistice with Germany by which France was divided into occupied and unoccupied zones. The German-occupied zone covered the north and west of the country, including the entire Atlantic coast, while the unoccupied zone consisted of the remaining two-fifths of the country in the south. This zone was now governed by an officially neutral French government led by Marshal Philippe Pétain, based in the city of Vichy in central France, 190 miles south of Paris. Hence, it was known as the Vichy government. It was also in charge of many civil functions in the northern occupied zone, as well as in the French colonial territories in North and Equatorial Africa and Southeast Asia. Of course, everyone knew that the Vichy government was nothing more than a German puppet state.

Given the situation in Western Europe, after much discussion, President Roosevelt and General Marshall decided to launch a massive coastal invasion of France to rout the German army. The plan was given the code name Operation Roundup, which the War Department and the president agreed should take place in the spring of 1943. Ike also agreed. He knew the Allies had to work together as a single unit on one plan if they were to defeat the Germans, the Italians, and the Japanese. Ike and his team began the preliminary planning for the attack. It would be a huge undertaking and involve the assembly of a massive force of British and American infantry and armored tank divisions, along with navy ships and airplanes. And it would all need to be mustered in the south of England, from where the invasion would begin. If Operation Roundup was a success, not only would it push the Germans out of France, but also it would take the pressure off Russian troops fighting the Germans on the Eastern Front.

As Ike worked on broad specifics for Operation Roundup, General Marshall left for a seven-day visit to London, where his aim was to persuade the British and other Allies to accept and commit to the operation. He also wanted to check in with the senior American military officer in the United Kingdom, General James Chaney.

When General Marshall returned to Washington, he told Ike that although the Allies had agreed to Operation Roundup, he doubted they really believed in it. He asked Ike to go to London and see what he made of the situation.

Ike was in London in early May. The first person he met with was Prime Minister Winston Churchill, who told Ike that the people of Great Britain could not endure a defeat in France and did not have enough troops to ensure a successful attack. Churchill instead thought that the Allied forces should invade North Africa and take the area back from the Germans and Italians. British general Bernard Montgomery echoed the prime minister's sentiment.

While Ike didn't agree with them, he understood their caution. During his time in France with the American Battle Monuments Commission, he'd walked many of the Great War battlefields and seen the devastation wrought upon the land. Hundreds of thousands of young Allied soldiers died fighting on those battlefields, and Ike knew that the leaders of Great Britain couldn't risk that happening again.

While in London, Ike also met with Lord Louis Mountbatten, commander of the Combined Operations Headquarters and a member of the British royal family. Of all the leaders Ike talked with in England, he got on best with him. Lord Mountbatten had a longstanding interest in technological advances in warfare. He had trained as a radio operator and even invented and patented an electronic device to help ships stay at specific distances from each other when traveling in convoy. Like Ike, Lord

Mountbatten was convinced that the military force that made the most use of these new advancements would win the war. Ike was glad to find a friend in Great Britain.

However, the main purpose of Ike's visit to London—to shore up British support for Operation Roundup—was a failure. Prime Minister Churchill and General Montgomery reiterated that the joint forces of the Allies should invade the North African coast. They argued that this would secure the Straits of Gibraltar, open up the Mediterranean Sea, and provide a steppingstone for the Allied invasion of Italy. Meanwhile, Lord Mountbatten was more eager to invade France, provided the Allies had enough ships and landing vehicles to do so.

Ike realized that working together presented many challenges. The British had already been at war for nearly three years against Germany and Italy, the Axis Powers. During this time their country had been bombed from the air on a number of occasions. Because of all of this, British military and political leaders wanted to have the final say as to where their troops would fight. Yet Ike knew that the US military would not accept giving up control of its own forces and accept British command. Somehow the two countries would have to find a way to make decisions together and trust each other to lead troops into battle.

By keeping his eyes and ears open in London, Ike learned that American troops already stationed there were not well liked by the British. They came across as boastful and indulgent, spending too much money while the residents of London were suffering under severe food and gas rations.

As he flew back to the United States, Ike was deeply disappointed. He hadn't been able to get everyone to agree on any one plan. He wondered how they were ever going to win the war if they could not agree on how to work together. Nor was Ike impressed with the work of General James Chaney, who didn't seem to grasp the urgency of getting things done. His men still worked office hours five days a week with weekends off, and they wore civilian clothes instead of uniforms and took long, leisurely lunch breaks.

On the return flight to Washington, Ike drafted some recommendations for General Marshall. Among them was recalling and replacing General Chaney and delaying Operation Roundup so they could all focus on an invasion of North Africa.

On June 11, 1942, Ike walked into General Marshall's office with a draft plan for the invasion of North Africa, which was now code-named Operation Torch. General Marshall looked up at Ike and asked, "In your opinion, are these plans as nearly complete as we can make them?"

"Yes, sir," Ike replied.

"Well, that's lucky," the general continued, "because you're the man who is going to carry them out. When can you leave?"

After a brief conversation, Ike left General Marshall's office needing to walk and think for a while. He could hardly believe what had just happened. He was going to be the top American commander in Europe. It took a while for it to sink in that he would be fully in charge of organizing, training, supplying, and commanding all American military forces operating in the European theater of war. He was also aware that his new position came with a challenge: this was the first time a single general had been placed in command over the various branches that formed the US military, and there were sure to be some ruffled feathers from commanders in the other service branches.

That night after dinner as Ike and Mamie relaxed over dessert and coffee, Ike told his wife, "I found out today that I'm being posted to London."

Mamie gulped. "What post are you going to have?"

"I'm going to command the whole shebang," Ike replied before going on to explain that General Marshall had given him ten days to wind up everything in the United States and get himself to London.

Ike had a lot to do in a short period of time. He had to prepare his successor at the War Department, say goodbye to John at West Point, spend time with Mamie, and clear his mind for the huge challenge he knew was ahead of him.

Four days later at his office Ike received another phone call from Mamie. Once more she had bad news to relay. Ike's younger brother Roy had died from a stroke at age forty-nine. Ike was shaken, and once again he didn't have time to mourn. The best he could do was send flowers and a card to his sister-in-law, Edna, and the four children.

Ike was grateful that his aides Mickey and Tex would be going with him to London. Over the time they'd been together, Ike had come to think of them as family. On Tuesday, June 23, 1942, a wet and blustery day, the airplane carrying Ike and his aides departed Bolling Field in Washington for the United Kingdom. When they landed safely in Prestwick, Scotland, Ike sent a telegram to Mamie saying, "The bird has landed. Because of you I've been the luckiest man in the world for twenty-six years—love Ike."

When he arrived in London on June 25, Ike knew he had to hit the ground running. So many things needed his immediate attention. He had to make sure American troops stationed in England respected their English counterparts, win over Britain's leaders and the public, and install a sense of urgency in the America military leaders under his command.

When Ike walked into the lobby of his new "home," he discovered the first thing that needed to change. Although Claridge's was the most exclusive hotel in London, it felt to Ike like an overstuffed funeral parlor. He needed something that felt like home, a place where he could relax in private. His aides soon found Telegraph Cottage, a country house with a garden, and rented it. The place was a forty-minute drive from US military headquarters, but Ike thought the peace and quiet it afforded was well worth the commute. Ike also bought a dog, a black terrier, whom he named Telex. He told people, "You can't talk war with a dog, and I'd like to have someone or something to talk to occasionally that doesn't know what the word means! A dog is my only hope."

Once settled into Telegraph Cottage, Ike set to work changing the British attitude toward the behavior of American soldiers stationed in their country. He held press conferences where he promised to be open with reporters and answer as many questions as possible. The British people immediately warmed to his smiling face and willingness to talk about difficult issues. Ike sent all American soldiers on guided bus trips around London so they could see firsthand the devastation the British people had already endured from the German bombing. He also made it clear that any American soldier who picked a fight with a British person or spoke disrespectfully to anyone would be sent straight back to the United States in disgrace. Ike was serious about the fact that to win this war the Americans and the British had to work together at all levels.

On July 7, 1942, after being in England for less than a month, Ike received word that he had been promoted to the rank of lieutenant general, making him a three-star general.

Working with the Allied military commanders was the most formidable challenge Ike had ever faced. He remembered General Fox Conner's words to him years before, "We cannot escape another great war. When we go into that war it will be in company with allies. . . . We must insist on individual and single responsibility—leaders will have to learn how to overcome nationalistic considerations in the conduct of campaigns."

In communiques with Ike, General Marshall made it clear he still believed a massive invasion of France followed by a direct push to Berlin was the Allies' best plan. Ike agreed, but no matter how hard he tried, the British were unwilling to commit large numbers of troops to such a plan. Then on July 22, President Roosevelt overrode General Marshall and gave a direct order that an Allied invasion of North Africa should begin in fall 1942. While Ike disagreed with the president, he'd received an order from his commander in chief and immediately pivoted to planning an invasion of France's Vichy-government-controlled territories in Northern Africa.

Ike and his team worked day and night refining the plan for Operation Torch, which they scheduled to begin in early November. The plan had two main goals. The first was to take control of the North African coast, which formed the southern coastline of the Mediterranean Sea, enabling it to be used as a steppingstone for the invasion of Italy. The second goal was to trap and destroy Italian and German forces that had been fighting the British in Egypt in an attempt to gain control of the Suez Canal. The enemy forces had come within two hundred miles of achieving their goals under the leadership of German tank commander Field Marshal Erwin Rommel before British forces managed to push them back into Italian-controlled Libya.

It was also hoped that Operation Torch would force Germany to move troops from the Eastern Front to North Africa to counter the attack, thus relieving some of the pressure on the Soviet military. The plan involved an initial attack by sea in three coastal areas: Casablanca in French Morocco, and Oran and Algiers in Algeria. No one knew if French Vichy forces stationed in these areas would stand down and join the Allies or fight to the death for the Axis. After landing and, if need be, subduing Vichy forces, the combined British and American forces would head east to trap, capture, and destroy Rommel's army.

On November 4, six B-17 Flying Fortresses carrying Ike and most of his staff took off from England for Gibraltar at the mouth of the Mediterranean Sea. A single German fighter plane attacked them on the way, but it was soon shot down. Upon arrival the team set up their command and communications headquarters for Operation Torch in Admiralty Tunnel, deep inside the Rock of Gibraltar.

On November 8, 1942, the outcome of Operation Torch lay in the hands of officers and the 107,000 American and British troops landing on the beaches of Morocco and Algeria. The thirty-three thousand men coming ashore in Morocco were all Americans who had traveled directly by sea from Virginia to make the landing. They were led by Ike's old friend, General George Patton. The two forces landing in Algeria were made up of American and British soldiers.

Upon landing on the beaches, the forces met little French Vichy opposition. As they began pushing forward, some of the French forces began to resist. But two days later Ike struck a bargain with French commanders that led to cooperation between them and the invading force. With the deal made, the combined forces moved quickly to consolidate their gains in Morocco and Algeria and head on to their second objective—trapping, capturing, and destroying

Rommel's forces. The German field marshal put up a far stronger fight than anticipated. He managed to escape the Allied pincer movement and spent the next three months tenaciously fighting the joint forces. However, the Allies cut supply lines to North Africa. The German and Italian troops could no longer go on, and they surrendered on May 6, 1943.

It had taken six months, longer than Ike originally hoped, but Operation Torch was a success. The Germans had been pushed out, and the Allies now controlled the plains and coastline of North Africa along the Mediterranean Sea, while Axis forces controlled the Mediterranean's northern coast. Now it was time for the Allies to turn their attention to invading Italy and taking control of that northern coast. Of course, Operation Torch had highlighted a number of weaknesses in the Allied forces and their battle plans. Ike intended to correct these as quickly as possible.

When Operation Torch was over, Ike flew over the southern coastline of the Mediterranean Sea with Harold Macmillan, his British political advisor. As they looked at the sea below, they observed a large Allied convoy sailing toward Egypt, safe from Axis attack.

"There, General," Macmillan said, "are the fruits of your victory."

Ike's eyes stung with tears as he turned to his political advisor. "*Ours*," he corrected. "You mean ours."

Chapter 14

Overlord

On July 10, 1943, two months after the Allies' success in North Africa, Ike oversaw the invasion of Sicily with a force of American, Canadian, British, and Free French troops and a combined fleet of 2,500 ships. The Allied soldiers stormed the beaches and within twenty-four hours took control of several cities in southern Sicily. The Germans and Italians defending the island were unable to repel the invasion, and on August 17 the Allies took control of Sicily, but not before most of the German troops had escaped to the Italian mainland.

Ike was disappointed that the Germans weren't captured, especially since they escaped while the American and British field commanders were preoccupied arguing with each other over their next moves. Nonetheless, he was encouraged by the way the American forces fought. They were no longer the rookies they had been when they arrived to fight in North Africa. They had learned from their mistakes and become seasoned and skilled units.

With Sicily under Allied control, British forces landed on the toe of mainland Italy on September 3, 1943, to begin the conquest. Almost immediately, Italy's king ordered the arrest of Italian leader Benito Mussolini, and the Italian government surrendered. Not so with their German Axis partners. With American forces having landed at Salerno, and British forces at Taranto, the German military units stationed in Italy put up a tenacious fight as the Allies fought their way up the center of Italy.

In December 1943 Ike was made Supreme Commander of Allied Expeditionary Forces in Europe. This meant he now had complete control of the Allied troops, more troops than any other commander in the history of the United States. In taking up the new position, Ike shifted his focus from Italy to planning an invasion of France's northern coast. The purpose of this was to drive German forces back until the Allies smashed them once and for all. The massive invasion, code-named Operation Overlord, would begin during spring 1944. It was an impossibly short amount of time to plan such a large operation, and General Marshall suggested Ike take a break before starting the job. When Ike disagreed, the general made it an order.

On December 31, 1943, Ike flew back to Washington for a secret rendezvous with Mamie and John. Virtually no one else knew he was back in the United

States other than top military leaders and President Roosevelt. Eighteen months had passed since Ike had flown out of Bolling Field for London. So much had happened in that time that Ike felt as if he'd been gone for years. He had left a two-star general and was returning a four-star one.

During his two weeks in the United States, Ike enjoyed two days alone with Mamie in a secluded cottage in Maryland that General Marshall had arranged for them. Ike made a secret visit to West Point to see John and visited his mother in Kansas. He also met a number of times with President Roosevelt and top military advisors at the White House.

Time at home passed quickly, and on January 14, 1944, Ike traveled back to England filled with nervous energy for what lay ahead. He was glad he'd chosen a talented team of Allied officers to help with the planning. Once back in England their full focus became Operation Overlord. France's Normandy coast was chosen for the invasion, and code names were assigned to the five beaches the Allies would land on—Utah, Omaha, Sword, Gold, and Juno. It would be the biggest offensive action ever launched, with 1,200 airplanes and more than five thousand ships and boats. While most of the 160,000 troops involved in the operation came from the United States, Great Britain, and Canada, battalions or individual soldiers from Australia, New Zealand, Greece, Free France, Belgium, Czechoslovakia, Denmark, the Netherlands, Norway, and Poland were also part of the force.

Ike estimated that following the invasion, by the

end of August 1944, the Allies would need over two million troops on the ground in France as they engaged the Germans in battle. All of the armies, navies, and air defenses involved in the operation needed to be precisely coordinated to allow everything and everyone to work together when Ike gave the order to invade. Everyone—from the weatherman to the quartermaster in charge of rations and the mechanics in charge of stocking enough spare tires for the Jeeps and motorcycles—had a vital part to play. If one thing was forgotten or miscalculated, men would pay with their lives.

During the planning, Ike coordinated some things he'd never dealt with before. He had a large number of men working on Operation Fortitude, whose objective was to spread false information to the Germans so they would think the Allies had more battalions and choose a different landing place and time. They created eight fake army divisions, which were supposedly in Scotland, waiting to attack Norway. Radio communications were sent to and from Scotland, while two hundred Bigbobs (flimsy rafts made of oil drums and canvas) were floated in the estuary of the river Thames to make it look like naval exercises were in preparation for a large-scale amphibious landing. Over a dozen German spies in England had defected, and they acted as double agents, feeding false information back to Nazi leaders.

That was just one of hundreds of actions going on simultaneously. All sorts of medical situations had to be considered. Hospitals across Britain were prepared to treat casualties from the landing in France, but the wounded would first need to be transported back across the English Channel, unloaded, evaluated, and taken by truck, ambulance, or train to the best hospital for them. Blood bank supply systems were set up to collect from the public the estimated 800,000 pints of plasma that would be needed during the first few days after D-Day, as the start day of the mass invasion was called.

Even providing enough maps for the invasion proved a mammoth task when the Allies realized they would need enough ink and paper to print 170 million top-secret copies. When printed, the maps weighed three thousand tons and had to be securely transported by armed guards.

Ike also had to figure out how to get heavy transport ships close enough to shore to unload their cargoes of military equipment and vehicles. Normally such ships would dock and unload in deepwater harbors, especially along the northern French coast, where the tide rose and fell twenty-two feet. But because the Germans firmly controlled all of France's harbors, the Allies would have to somehow make harbors for their ships.

Plans were soon underway to create two artificial harbors, code-named Mulberries. One would be off Omaha Beach, where American forces would land, and the other would be farther east at Gold Beach, where British and Canadian forces would come ashore. To make the Mulberries, a formation of old ships lined up bow-to-stern would be scuttled close to shore. Large concrete caissons constructed along Britain's southern coast would then be towed across the English Channel and sunk close to the ships. Large floating piers would be put in place for ships to dock against and unload their cargo. Long floating roadways would connect these piers to the beach. All of this required engineering precision, and Ike was glad the project was being guided by a team of skilled British engineers.

There was also a question about whether armored tanks would bog down on the beach. Sand samples from the beaches were needed to evaluate this. A British submarine transported two royal engineers to the French coast, where they made a daring foray onto Gold Beach under cover of darkness to collect buckets of sand for analysis.

Another crucial decision was the timing of the invasion. Ike wanted to invade at dawn to surprise the Germans. Assuming that everyone was ready and the sea calm, two vital factors had to align: the tide and the moonlight. A full moon was needed to provide enough light for paratroopers and troops in gliders to land behind enemy lines at 4:00 a.m. and for an early morning naval bombardment. Also the men needed to go ashore at low tide so they could see and destroy the German mines and barriers erected on the beaches. The rising incoming tide would ensure that landing vessels wouldn't become stranded on the beach. According to tide and weather data, the best date for the invasion was June 5, 1944, though it could be stretched one or two days later if the weather was bad.

This was the first combat experience for most American troops arriving to participate in Operation

Overlord. Most of them were young, with over half under twenty years of age. A large-scale war exercise was planned for the troops who would be landing at Utah Beach. As in the Big One in Louisiana nearly three years before, Ike knew there would probably be loss of life during the exercise. However, nothing could have prepared him for this body count. On April 27, 1944, six weeks before D-Day, the mock amphibious landing took place at Slapton Beach on England's Devon coast. Before the exercise was over, nearly a thousand American soldiers were dead. Some were killed because of a friendly-fire misunderstanding when the first group landed on the beach. The rest died when, after dark, agile German torpedo boats, called E-boats, attacked a convoy of tank landing ships headed to Slapton Beach. Two of the ships sank, and two more were severely damaged.

Ike realized it was vital that word of the incident not get out, at least not until after D-Day. If it did, morale would plummet, and the Germans would gain a lot of information about the operation. Ike sent out a memo stating that anyone who said a word about the incident would be immediately court-martialed. Ike and his staff learned two important lessons from the mishap. The first was that the British and the Americans were not using the same radio frequencies and so were unable to communicate with each other. The second was that many of the men had drowned on the sunken ships because they wore their life vests around their waists instead of putting them on properly. While Ike knew that wearing life vests properly was difficult given the heavy combat packs troops carried, the simple action would have saved hundreds of lives. As a result, radio frequencies across all forces were standardized, and troops traveling in amphibious landing craft were given thorough instructions on buckling their life vests tightly across their chests before boarding the boats. In addition, plans were drawn up for small craft to pick up floating survivors on D-Day.

On Monday, May 15, Ike's official Cadillac staff car pulled to a halt outside St. Paul's School in the heart of London. General Montgomery and his staff had taken over the building, and Ike had to present his top-secret invitation at the door in order to be let in. Although he was easily recognizable, orders were that no one got inside without an invitation.

A group of 145 men, including King George VI of England, Prime Minister Winston Churchill, every principal cabinet member of the British chiefs of staff and the War Cabinet, and the Allied generals, were in the school auditorium. It was the most impressive military gathering Ike had ever attended. They had come together to finalize plans for Operation Overlord. As he walked in, Ike wondered what would happen to their plans if the place was bombed at that moment.

The centerpiece of the room was a thirty-foot-wide tilted platform on which sat a huge papier-mâché model of the southern coast of England and northern coast of France. Standing beside it was a man with a long pointer. His job was to walk over the map in his socks and point out the locations being discussed. Ike needed to be sure everyone knew his exact role and how it fit into the overall plan. This was the last chance for anyone to voice his doubts or point out any flaws he saw in the plan, and Ike urged them all to speak up. King George VI and Prime Minister Churchill both gave speeches reminding them all that they were dependent upon one another.

Outwardly Ike always tried to look confident in front of his men, but inwardly he was anxious about every detail. Right then his biggest concern was the weather. For the invasion to take place, the sea had to be calm enough for navy ships to get close enough to bombard the coast and for the amphibious landing craft to reach the beaches. The winds also had to be low so that airplanes could swoop in over the coast and bomb German gun emplacements and provide cover for the troops hitting the beaches.

Along the southern coast of England, 133,000 Allied troops were encamped. It was time for Ike to order the camps sealed to guard the secret that the final preparations and the loading of ships for Operation Overlord were beginning.

On June 1 Ike moved the Supreme Headquarters Allied Expeditionary Force (SHAEF) to an advance command post located at Southwick House, just north of Portsmouth. Most planners and leaders of Operation Overlord stayed in the manor house. As a precaution, Ike chose to set up camp in the woods about a mile from Southwick House in case the Germans learned the secret of what was going on there. As well as a tent and a trailer for Ike to sleep in, the campsite had a direct telephone connection to the White House in Washington.

At 4:00 a.m. on June 4, 1944, Ike walked the mile from his camp to Southwick House. Stars shone above and not a leaf rustled in the birch trees. Inside the large manor house, Ike felt the tension in the air as he sat down and nodded for Group Captain James Stagg, Operation Overlord's meteorologist, to brief them all. Ike noted the grim expression on the meteorologist's face. He quickly learned the source of it. Despite the weather looking calm and perfect for the invasion at that moment, Captain Stagg said a huge storm—the fiercest in the month of June in over fifty years—was brewing to the north of them. By D-Day morning, the storm's full fury would be unleashed on the English and French coastlines. Ike looked out the window at the still, moonlit predawn. It was hard to imagine that the weather could deteriorate so completely in twenty-four hours. Still, because he'd watched Captain Stagg carefully and knew he was good at his job, he ordered a twenty-four-hour postponement of Operation Overlord.

It was a difficult decision. Men and ships were already in position and would have to be recalled, increasing the chance of the invasion plans being detected. In addition, the sailors manning the midget submarines that would guide ships to the various beaches were already in place. They would have to stay submerged and undetected in enemy waters for another twenty-four hours.

The following morning, June 5, Ike was awake again before four o'clock. This time he awoke to the sound of howling wind and torrential rain. As he opened his trailer door, he was equal parts grateful he'd ordered the postponement and concerned that the chance of launching D-Day in June might be gone. This time he allowed himself to be driven to Southwick House. Inside, the same group of men waited silently as huge gusts of wind shook the house and rattled the windows.

Despite the foul weather, Ike thought he detected a slight smile on Captain Stagg's face. "Gentlemen," the captain began in his Scottish accent, "there will be a high front passing over England later today. It will push the storm farther south. This is good news. I calculate there will be a window of good weather of between twenty-four and thirty-six hours starting early tomorrow morning."

Ike sat for a long minute, watching the rain pellet the windows. How much did he trust the Scottish captain? The lives of millions of soldiers under his command rested on the answer. At last he stood and said simply, "Okay, we'll go."

Suddenly the room was alive with activity and noise. A myriad of things needed to be activated. There was no going back. In twenty hours the first air bombing of the French coast would begin, followed several hours later by the first troops attempting to land on the beaches.

Ike fingered the press release he'd written. It read in part, "Our landings . . . have failed. . . . I have withdrawn the troops. My decision to attack at this time and place was based upon the best information available. . . . If any blame or fault attaches to the attempt, it is mine alone." He folded the sheet of paper and slipped it into his pocket. The plans for the battle were laid. In a few hours the effectiveness of those plans would be judged by the success or failure in achieving their goal.

Ike's mind drifted to his family for a moment. Mamie and her parents were traveling to West Point for John's graduation the following day. Ike hoped that when Mamie heard news of the invasion, she wouldn't let anxiety ruin her celebration with John. Throughout the remainder of the day, Ike kept busy encouraging his officers and visiting the troops already loaded onto Allied ships in Portsmouth Harbor.

At 10:30 p.m. Ike visited the 101st Airborne Division at Newbury, a short drive to the north. In just a few hours the airplanes carrying these men would take off for France. Ike was aware of the grim prediction that half of these soldiers would probably be killed in action. He talked and joked with the men, who were already in camouflage and had their faces blackened with a mixture of cocoa and linseed oil for battle. Each man had a copy of a letter Ike had penned. It had been distributed to each soldier, sailor, and airman of the Allied Expeditionary Force. It read,

> You are about to embark upon the Great Crusade, toward which we have striven these many months. The eyes of the world are upon you. The hope and prayers of liberty-loving people everywhere march with you. In company with our brave Allies and brothers-in-arms on other Fronts, you will bring about the destruction of the German war machine,

the elimination of Nazi tyranny over the oppressed peoples of Europe, and security for ourselves in a free world.

Your task will not be an easy one. Your enemy is well trained, well equipped and battle-hardened. He will fight savagely.

But this is the year 1944! Much has happened since the Nazi triumphs of 1940–41. The United Nations have inflicted upon the Germans great defeats, in open battle, man-to-man. Our air offensive has seriously reduced their strength in the air and their capacity to wage war on the ground.

Our Home Fronts have given us an overwhelming superiority in weapons and munitions of war, and placed at our disposal great reserves of trained fighting men. The tide has turned! The free men of the world are marching together to Victory!

I have full confidence in your courage, devotion to duty and skill in battle. We will accept nothing less than full Victory!

Good luck! And let us beseech the blessing of Almighty God upon this great and noble undertaking.

As he gave the men a final salute, one of the paratroopers yelled to Ike, "Quit worrying, General. We'll take care of this for you."

Ike wiped away tears as he climbed back into his staff car. War was hard and brutal; he knew that. He consoled himself with the fact he'd done everything he could to ensure the greatest gains for the Allies while costing the fewest lives possible. What had to be done, had to be done, and these men, Ike was sure, would live in his memory forever, along with all of the other regular soldiers involved in the fighting. They would always be the true heroes of the war.

Chapter 15

I Like Ike

Three weeks after Allied forces landed on Normandy's beaches, Ike stood on French soil. The D-Day fighting had been fierce. About ten thousand Allied soldiers were killed or wounded. None of the initial assault forces managed to secure their first-day objectives. But in the following days they fought their way inland from the landing beaches and took control of the surrounding countryside to establish an Allied foothold in continental Europe. Ike knew it was just the beginning. Many more battles lay ahead as the Allies advanced to liberate France and press on into Germany. Returning to London after his visit, Ike had no doubt the Allies would win the war. This was the beginning of the end of Nazi Germany.

Ike began highlighting red-letter victory days in his diary. On June 26 the French port of Cherbourg was liberated from the Germans, on July 21 Caen was liberated, and August 25 marked the liberation of Paris. There were also bad days when battles didn't go as planned, but the Allies were still able to push German forces back toward Germany.

On December 16, 1944, Ike was promoted to the rank of five-star general. This was a newly created rank, and it was also awarded to George Marshall, Douglas MacArthur, and Henry "Hap" Arnold. Ike couldn't take time to celebrate the promotion, because the same day, the Germans launched a massive counterattack against advancing Allied forces in western Belgium, northeast France, and Luxembourg. Once more the fighting was fierce, and nearly ninety thousand Allied soldiers were killed or wounded. But on January 25, 1945, the Allies were victorious over the Germans in the battle. The Allied push into Germany continued, with the forces under Ike's command moving in from the west and the Soviet army moving in from the east.

On April 12, 1945, President Franklin Roosevelt died of a brain hemorrhage, and Vice President Harry S. Truman was sworn in as president of the United States. Ike was sorry President Roosevelt hadn't lived to see the end of the war, which he was sure wasn't far off now that Allied forces had penetrated deep into Germany.

On May 1 Germany's capital, Berlin, fell to the Soviet army. The following day came news that Adolf Hitler had committed suicide in his Berlin bunker two days earlier as Soviet forces approached. On May 7, 1945, German generals arrived at Ike's command headquarters at Reims in northeast France, where they tendered the unconditional surrender of the German armed forces to the Allies. Once the surrender documents were signed, Ike sent an official message to Allied leaders stating simply, "The mission of this Allied Force was fulfilled at 0241, local time, May 7th, 1945."

The following day church bells rang out across Europe and the United States—the war in Europe was over. Adolf Hitler was dead, and Germany had surrendered. The Allies dubbed May 8, 1945, V-E Day for Victory in Europe. The war in the East still raged on, though General Douglas MacArthur was quickly closing in on Japan and gearing up to invade the country. It would be only a matter of time before the Japanese also capitulated to the Allies.

Following V-E Day, control of Germany was divided among the Allies: the Soviet Union, the United States, Great Britain, and France. President Truman appointed Ike to serve as commander of American-occupied Germany. While carrying out his new assignment, Ike learned that President Truman had okayed the use of a newly developed weapon—the atomic bomb. On August 6 the first of these bombs was dropped on the Japanese city of Hiroshima, and three days later another was dropped on Nagasaki. Given the amount of devastation and number of civilian deaths the bombs caused, Ike wasn't sure that using them was a wise choice. He believed that because Japan was so weakened by years of war, surrender was inevitable. Nonetheless, soon after the bombing, Japanese Emperor Hirohito surrendered his country to the Allies. World War II at last was over.

When he made a trip back to the United States to talk with President Truman and meet with Congress, Ike was greeted with fanfare and huge parades. He found it all a little embarrassing but realized he was the face of victory to millions of people in the United States and across the world.

In November 1945, General George Marshall resigned as US Army chief of staff, and Ike was named his successor. After three and a half years in Europe, it was time to return home. Once in Washington, Ike and Mamie moved into Quarters 1 at Fort Meyer, across the Potomac River in Arlington, Virginia. Since 1910 this twenty-one-room house had been the official residence of the US Army chief of staff.

At first it was challenging for Ike and Mamie to adjust to living together again. They'd both led such different lives during the war. But with love and determination, they once more became a happy couple. Ike was glad to have Mamie's support, as his new job was extremely challenging.

In mid-September 1946, Ike received a phone call from his brother Milton informing him their eighty-four-year-old mother, Ida, had died. Ike was glad he'd visited her several times since the war ended. Unlike at his father's death three months after the Pearl Harbor attack, Ike and Mamie were able to return to Abilene, Kansas, for Ida's funeral. After the funeral, Ike and his brothers donated the family home to the newly formed Eisenhower Foundation on condition they kept it exactly as their mother had left it.

Ike's son John, now an army captain, had been assigned to duty in Vienna, Austria. The following summer he took leave to return to the United States to marry Barbara Thompson, whom he'd met in Vienna. Barbara was the daughter of Colonel Percy Walter Thompson, who was also stationed there. Ike and Mamie helped them arrange a military wedding that was held at the Old Point Comfort Chapel at Fort Monroe, Virginia, on June 10, 1947.

Ike had agreed to serve as US Army chief of staff for two years. When that time was up, he was exhausted. He thought about what he wanted to do next. He was persuaded to write a memoir of his war experiences. He hired three secretaries who took turns taking down his words in shorthand as he dictated them and afterward typed them up. Using his war diaries, letters, and maps, Ike worked from seven in the morning until eleven at night on the project, taking short breaks for meals. At the end of three months, he'd produced a 250,000-word book, which he titled *Crusade in Europe*. The book was rushed into print and became an instant bestseller.

After completing the book, Ike and Mamie were overjoyed to welcome their first grandchild, a boy named Dwight David Eisenhower II.

On June 7, 1948, Ike took up the position of president of Columbia University in New York City. He and Mamie moved into the president's mansion and began the next phase of their life together.

Both Ike and Mamie dreamed of someday retiring

to a country home, and during this time they begin searching for a house to buy. In the end they settled on a dilapidated farmhouse on a 189-acre property in Gettysburg, Pennsylvania. Their friends the Allens had recently bought a farm there, and Ike liked the idea of returning to the Camp Colt area where he, Mamie, and Ikky had lived for a time years before. Ike and Mamie visited their new property on weekends and talked together about how they wanted to renovate the farmhouse to suit their needs.

Ike soon realized that being a university president involved many meetings and policy debates as well as constant fundraising, especially since he was such a well-recognized and revered public figure. What the job didn't provide Ike was the contact he'd hoped for with students attending Columbia University.

In October 1950, as Ike went about his duties at Columbia, President Truman summoned him to the White House to inform him he had a new job for him. Ike was the unanimous choice to become supreme commander of the newly formed North Atlantic Treaty Organization (NATO). The United States, Canada, and ten Western European countries had formed the organization to establish a joint defensive military force.

At the end of World War II, Europe was divided along an east-west split, with free states in the west and Soviet-dominated Communist states in the east. The Soviet Union continued to maintain its military forces at wartime levels, while the United States rapidly decreased the size of its wartime army. This led to ten times more Soviet soldiers stationed in Europe than American soldiers. The Soviet Union also showed no sign of leaving the countries it had invaded during the war. Because of this, NATO was formed to build a unified military force in Western Europe that could counter the Soviets.

Ike realized that taking command of NATO would be a challenging job, as so many questions still needed to be answered: Would NATO be a multinational military force or an alliance of independent national armies? And how many American troops would need be stationed in Western Europe?

Soon after visiting the White House, Ike and Mamie headed to Paris, where NATO was headquartered, for Ike to serve as its supreme commander. In February 1951, Ike visited Washington, DC, to brief the president and Congress on how NATO was developing.

During his visit home Ike learned that many people wanted him to run for president of the United States. He was surprised by this. Like most members of the armed forces, he'd never voted in an election, a tradition underscoring the fact that members of the military didn't take sides in politics. Their job was to support and serve the elected government regardless of the political party they represented. Ike had taken the tradition so seriously that no one was sure whether he was a Republican or a Democrat. He soon had offers from both parties to become their presidential candidate. President Truman offered to step aside at the next election in favor of Ike's being the Democrats' nominee. Meanwhile one of Ike's friends urged him to seek the Republican nomination against Senator Robert Taft of Ohio, who was considered a weak candidate. Ike was unconvinced and returned to Paris and his work with NATO.

The momentum for Ike to run for president didn't die down, and later in the year Senator Henry Cabot Lodge of Massachusetts visited Paris and urged Ike to run for president as a Republican. Ike was noncommittal. In January 1952 Senator Lodge announced that Ike was a Republican and entered his name onto the New Hampshire primary ballot as one. He even had a simple campaign slogan for him: "I Like Ike." In Paris Ike remained silent until the results of the March primary vote were made public. Senator Robert Taft, who had campaigned vigorously, won 38 percent of the vote, while Ike, who had done no direct campaigning, won 50 percent. A week later, in the Minnesota primary, Ike received more than 106,000 write-in votes. At the end of April, President Truman announced he would not seek another term. Ike began to think that running for president was his next step.

On June 1, 1952, Ike resigned from NATO and returned to the United States to pursue the Republican nomination for president. At the Republican National Convention held in Chicago July 7–11, Ike was chosen as the party's presidential candidate by a wide margin. At the convention he was paired with Richard Nixon, a young senator from California, as his vice-presidential running mate.

Following the convention, either separately or together, Ike and Richard Nixon crisscrossed the country campaigning, pointing out that if they won, they would end the Democrats' twenty-year hold on the White House. Huge crowds flocked to see Ike, some because he was a presidential candidate and others because he was a war hero.

When the votes were tallied on election day, November 4, 1952, Ike had been swept into office with the largest popular vote for president in American history. Not only that, but for the first time in twenty-four years, Republicans also held a majority in both houses of Congress.

On Tuesday, January 20, 1953, General Dwight D. Eisenhower was sworn in as the thirty-fourth president of the United States. He took the oath of office with his hand resting on the Bible his mother had given him when he left for West Point. He added the words "So help me God" at the end of the oath. Ike also did something no newly elected president had done before. He asked the crowd to bow their heads and pray with him for a blessing on the nation. He knew this would surprise many people. He was not a regular churchgoer and rarely talked about religion. But in Paris he'd met American evangelist Billy Graham and spent time with him. As a result of their meetings, Ike's view on God had softened. Ike now felt comfortable sharing his private prayer with the world.

Following a luncheon with leaders of both houses of Congress, Ike stood on a stage with Mamie and the Nixons and watched the inauguration parade, which stretched for ten miles and involved thirty thousand participants. Three-quarters of a million people lined the streets of Washington to see the parade, and half of all Americans watched it on television, many having bought their first TV set in order to do so. The parade took four and a half hours to review, and Ike stood tall watching every minute of it. Among his favorite participants in the procession were the cadets from West Point. It took him back forty years to when, as a cadet, he had marched in President Wilson's inauguration parade.

The next day, Ike and Mamie moved into the White House to begin another chapter in their lives. In typical style, Ike had already made the key appointments in his administration, gathering forty top people in their fields to aid and advise him.

Throughout the campaign Ike had continued to meet with evangelist Billy Graham, who encouraged him to become a member of a church. On February 1, 1953, just ten days after being sworn in as president, Ike was baptized and confirmed in a private ceremony at the National Presbyterian Church. Mamie, who had been raised Presbyterian, had already been baptized. Ike was determined to attend church every Sunday that he possibly could.

One of the first issues Ike faced was racial segregation, an issue he had little experience with. As a boy growing up in Abilene, Kansas, he hadn't known any black people, and since the army was segregated he had never trained with any either. While Ike personally believed fairness and equality should extend to all people in the United States, he felt it a bad idea for the federal government to tell states what they could or could not do. But he realized he could set an example. As president, Ike had authority over Washington and all military bases. President Truman had begun the process of desegregating the armed forces, and Ike sped it up. He also championed desegregating the nation's capital, making it illegal to refuse service to black people there.

Ike also surprised many people by speaking out against increasing the military budget. In his speech entitled "Chance for Peace," he pointed out the opportunities to improve people's lives that would be lost for every new tank or airplane that was purchased for the military.

At the same time Ike looked for ways to modernize America. On May 13, 1954, he signed the Wiley-Dander Seaway Act into law. Jointly with Canada, this act called for the creation of the St. Lawrence Seaway, a canal, lock, and river system that would allow ships from the Atlantic Ocean to sail along the St. Lawrence River and on into the Great Lakes.

Meanwhile, Mamie balanced her duties as first lady with overseeing the renovations of their Gettysburg farmhouse. When the renovations were complete, on July 1, 1955, their thirty-ninth wedding anniversary, Ike and Mamie held a huge housewarming party. They invited the entire White House domestic staff, including the telephone operators and janitors, to celebrate with them.

By September 1955 things were going well in the United States. The economy was booming, there were no major crises in the world, and Ike's approval rating among Americans was at 79 percent. Ike and Mamie decided to vacation in Denver, where they stayed at Mamie's mother's house. During the vacation Ike suffered a heart attack. He was whisked to Fitzsimons Army Medical Hospital in a Secret Service car for treatment.

The next morning newspaper headlines around the country blared the news of his illness. Uncertain whether the president would live or die, the stock market recorded its worst single-day loss since the start of World War II. Reporters swarmed the hospital for any news or photographs they could get. At first, Ike's physicians tried to conceal his condition. Ike, though, disagreed and instructed his press secretary, Jim Hagerty, to "tell them everything." Dr. Paul White, a leading cardiologist, was called in from Harvard University to attend to Ike. After examining him, Dr. White announced that Ike had a good chance for recovery. He was right. Within two weeks Ike could once again sign official papers and even hosted dignitaries in his hospital room.

During his illness Ike received thousands of cards and gifts from well-wishers. He gave most of the gifts away, but he kept one—a pair of maroon pajamas from the White House press corps. They had embroidered "Much Better Thanks" on the left pocket and five stars on the collar. Dr. White ordered a sixth star to be sewn on for "good conduct."

Ike spent his sixty-fifth birthday in the hospital, and on November 11, he was released. Eleven days later he held his next cabinet meeting at the presidential retreat in Maryland, which he had named Camp David after his grandson.

Ike continued to feel stronger, and just before

Christmas 1955 he and Mamie welcomed their fourth grandchild, a girl, whom John and Barbara named Mary.

In early 1956 Ike was back to working on the Federal Aid Highway Act. Ever since participating in the 1919 Motor Transport Corps Convoy across the United States, Ike had been observing that the country didn't have a good highway system. And every year there were more cars on the road—fifty-four million of them in 1955, twice as many as before the war. All predictions said that the number of cars would keep increasing. When he was in Germany, Ike had been able to travel long distances on wide, straight, divided highways. Now, as president, he was concerned that if the United States were to be hit by an atomic bomb, current roads would be inadequate to evacuate cities. As well, military bases in the country were not connected by good roads. The Federal Aid Highway Act would provide twenty-five billion dollars of federal funding for the construction of forty-one thousand miles of interstate highway over a ten-year period. It would be the largest public works project in American history. Ike did all he could to encourage Congress to pass the bill, and on June 29, 1956, he signed it into law. It had been a herculean effort getting it passed, but Ike was sure it would make life easier for countless Americans and improve the country's military defenses.

Americans seemed to agree with Ike, and in August they nominated him to run for a second term as president. Once again Richard Nixon was his running mate. When the votes were counted, the result was a landslide. Ike received over 57 percent of the popular vote and won forty-one of the forty-eight states in the Electoral College. He had earned himself another four years in the White House as president.

Chapter 16

End of an Era

On Monday, January 21, 1957, Ike was sworn in as president of the United States for a second term. As he took the oath of office, he realized that the nation and the world faced many challenges. Just before election day, Great Britain, France, and Israel had joined forces to attack Egypt and seize the Suez Canal. This had led the Soviet Union to support Egypt. Ike was disappointed in his old allies, particularly the British for not informing him beforehand of their proposed actions. He'd already issued warnings to the Allies and the Soviets about not escalating the situation further. He hoped it would be enough to ease tensions in the region. Of course, relations between the United States and the Soviet Union remained challenging. Both sides were involved in what was being called the Cold War, each trying to top the other by producing bigger and better weapons, particularly nuclear bombs, as well as seeking to check each other's foreign policy initiatives. Ike's hope during his second term was to find a way to de-escalate tensions between the two countries.

Although Ike had won another presidential term by a landslide, the Republican Party as a whole had not done so well. Both the Senate and House of Representatives were firmly under the control of Democrats. This meant that Ike would have to convince them to support the platforms he'd run on during the election. That could be difficult, though he was a master negotiator and sensed that the Democrats genuinely wanted to work with him for the good of the country.

On September 9, 1957, Ike signed the Civil Rights Act into law. This was the first civil rights bill to pass Congress since Reconstruction. The bill established the Civil Rights Division within the Justice Department, made it illegal to interfere with another citizen's right to vote, and created a six-member Civil Rights Commission to investigate allegations of voting rights abuse.

As Ike signed the Civil Rights Act, another civil rights issue erupted in Little Rock, Arkansas. Governor Orval Faubus sent the Arkansas National Guard to stop nine black high school students from enrolling in and attending segregated Little Rock High School. This was in direct violation of the Supreme Court's historic *Brown v. Board of Education* decision of May 17, 1954. This decision declared that laws establishing segregated schools were unconstitutional and thus schools throughout the nation must be desegregated.

After the decision was handed down during his first term as president, Ike was patient with Southern governors, allowing them time to develop plans to desegregate their schools. Now with the situation in Little Rock, Ike felt it was time for him to act. He dispatched the 101st Airborne Division to Little Rock and put the Arkansas National Guard under federal control with orders to enforce the Supreme Court decision. Seeing this federal show of force, Governor Faubus backed down, and the black high school students enrolled in and began attending the previously all-white school.

The following month, a crisis of a different sort gripped the nation. On October 4, 1957, Americans tuned in their radios to hear a strange beep-beep-beep sound. It was the sound of a radio signal emanating from a Soviet beach-ball-sized satellite named Sputnik orbiting the earth. For the first time in history, humans had launched something high enough to defy gravity and circle the earth. Ike wasn't taken by surprise. He knew that the Soviets had started a rocket program right after World War II and were ahead of the United States in getting into space. The American people, however, were in shock. Because they believed that their country was the most productive and scientifically advanced nation on earth, they found it hard to believe that the Soviet Union, which many thought technologically backward, had built a rocket sophisticated enough to carry a satellite into space. They wondered what the Soviets might be able to do next: build a satellite that could take photos of them from space? Or carry missiles to shoot at the United States? Perhaps they might somehow even send a man into space? The news media reported story after story about Sputnik and Soviet space aspirations, stirring hysteria within the United States.

Ike knew he had to do something to calm the nation. He decided that the United States needed a new agency to drive research into rockets and space at a much faster pace. He asked his science advisor, James R. Killian Jr., to convene the Presidential Science Advisory Committee to consider what to do and come up with recommendations. The committee's deliberations led to a bill establishing the National Aeronautics and Space Agency. Ike sent the bill to Congress on April 2, 1958, for consideration. After congressional hearings during the spring, some amendments were made to the bill, which was then passed and signed into law by Ike on July 29, 1958. The United States now had its own space agency, NASA, as everyone began calling it, to drive American space exploration forward.

Next Ike proposed the National Defense Education Act that would provide federal funding to help graduate more and better-qualified scientists and engineers. The act aimed to give scholarships and loans to students who studied science, mathematics, and modern foreign languages. The House Democrats agreed with Ike, saying in their report, "It is no exaggeration to say that America's progress in many fields of endeavor in the years ahead—in fact, the very survival of our free country—may depend in large part upon the education we provide for our young people now."

While many Americans were unsettled by the Soviet Union and the Cold War nuclear one-upmanship in which the two countries were engaged, Ike insisted it was possible to work toward peace and understanding between the two nations. To further this, he invited Soviet premier Nikita Khrushchev to visit the United States. Khrushchev and his family arrived in Washington on September 15, 1959. Ike welcomed them, after which the Soviet premier spent the next thirteen days touring the country, including a movie studio in Los Angeles and a farm in Iowa. Ike and Mamie also hosted a state dinner for Khrushchev at the White House. By the time the premier's visit to the United States was over, he and Ike had built trust between each other and forged an understanding about how the two countries might achieve détente. To explore this, they scheduled a summit meeting in Paris for May 1960.

In 1947, Congress had passed a law that restricted the president of the United States to serving only two terms in the office. This meant that Ike would retire in January 1961. He began thinking about how he could best use his influence during his last two years as president. Although he was sixty-eight years old, he decided to set out on a series of goodwill tours to various places around the world to promote friendship and better communication with the

United States. He was sure this would also play a part in curbing the Soviet Union's influence in other countries.

In December 1959, Ike embarked upon an eleven-day tour of Asia and the Middle East. Since Mamie didn't like to fly, Ike took his son, John, and daughter-in-law, Barbara, with him. They traveled in the new Boeing 707-120 Stratoliner jet aircraft the US Air Force had purchased to transport the president. Because it carried the president, the plane was designated Air Force One.

It was the first time a sitting US president had visited many of the countries where they made stops. Everywhere he went, Ike was greeted by enormous crowds. In Karachi, Pakistan, over three-quarters of a million people lined the streets to wave and catch a glimpse of him. And five-story-high banners bearing the image of Ike's face were stretched across buildings. Television crews followed the president during the trip, capturing various moments that were shown on the news back in the United States.

After nineteen days of travel, Ike arrived back in Washington in time for Christmas. A large crowd gathered at Lafayette Square in front of the White House to welcome him home with a spectacular candlelight vigil.

Two months later Ike was off again, this time to Latin America. He spent a hectic fourteen days meeting with presidents of the various countries he visited and making forty official speeches.

In 1960, an election year, since Ike couldn't serve as president again, the Republican party needed a new candidate to run for office. They chose Vice President Richard Nixon, with Henry Cabot Lodge, former US ambassador to the United Nations, as Nixon's running mate. The Democrats selected forty-two-year-old Senator John F. Kennedy of Massachusetts as their nominee and Texas Senator Lyndon Johnson as Kennedy's running mate. Ike referred to Kennedy as a "young whippersnapper," who he believed had impractical ideas and little understanding of how to manage something as complex as the US government.

In mid-May 1960 Ike flew to Paris, where the planned summit conference with Soviet Premier Nikita Khrushchev was due to start on the sixteenth. Regrettably, all the goodwill Ike had worked hard to build between the United States and the Soviet Union was dashed when the Soviet premier learned that an American U-2 spy plane had been shot down flying over the Soviet Union. Aerial spying was a violation of an early agreement Ike and Khrushchev had made, and now the United States had been caught at it. The Soviet premier walked out of the summit when Ike refused to apologize for the incident. It was a shattering defeat. Ike had put a great deal of thought and energy into working toward a peaceful coexistence with the Soviets. The incident also gave John F. Kennedy a new reason to criticize Republican foreign policy.

Forty-seven years had passed since Arizona was admitted to the Union as the forty-eighth state, and during 1959 Ike had the privilege of signing the proclamations that admitted Alaska and Hawaii as the forty-ninth and fiftieth states. In June 1960 Ike decided to visit both states to personally welcome them into the Union. He set out on a two-week tour that took him to Anchorage, Alaska; Wake Island; the Philippines; Taiwan; and Honolulu, Hawaii. The highlight of the trip was his stop in Manila, where Philippine President Carlos Garcia greeted him at the airport along with a thunderous twenty-one-gun salute. Ike was then guided to a podium, where he made a brief speech. His voice trembled as he began. "It's a homecoming for me. As I look at these familiar sights there is one thing, of course, that is missing. So many of my old friends of the years just preceding World War II are gone. So many of them paid the price free men have been called upon to pay again and again for the defense of freedom."

The Filipino president then gave his own speech before the two men climbed into an open-top limousine for the ten-mile drive to Malacañang Palace, where Ike would be staying. Ike was overwhelmed when he learned that two million Filipinos had lined the route to the palace, many of them waiting for hours just to welcome him back as the limousine passed. As he entered Malacañang Palace, Ike thought back to the lunches he'd enjoyed there while playing bridge with President Manuel Quezon thirty-five years before.

The next day Ike enjoyed a reunion with friends he'd known from his time stationed in the Philippines. At his request these included everyone from retired army officers to his old driver. He wished Mamie could have been there with him. Together they could have visited their old home, the Manila Hotel, and watched another beautiful sunset across Manila Bay.

Two months after returning from the trip, Ike and Mamie experienced the end of an era when Mamie's mother died in September 1960. Mamie and her sister Mike packed up the old family home in Denver, where Ike and Mamie had been married forty-four years before and where they'd stayed many times over the years.

As the election campaign moved into its final two weeks, the polls showed a close race, with John F. Kennedy slightly ahead of Nixon. Ike made a vigorous effort to campaign for Richard Nixon during the last ten days before the election.

On November 8, 1960, the nation voted. When the votes were counted, two-tenths of 1 percent separated the two candidates in the popular vote, but Kennedy won with the Electoral College vote 303 to 219. At forty-three years of age, he had made history, becoming the youngest US president ever elected and the first Roman Catholic one.

Ike and Mamie invited their son John, Barbara, and their four grandchildren to experience one last Christmas in the White House. The next year the Kennedys would be hosting their own Christmas festivities there.

On January 19, 1961, the eve of Kennedy's inauguration, Democrats were at balls celebrating and Ike and Mamie sat upstairs in the private wing of the White House eating dinner. Their time as first couple of the most powerful country in the world had ended. The next day, at seventy years of age, Dwight Eisenhower would pass the torch of leadership of the United States to a man born the same year as their son Ikky.

Ike and Mamie talked quietly of the changes ahead of them and the chance to be out of the spotlight of public service that had consumed their lives for five decades. Ike looked forward to developing a prize-winning herd of Angus cows on his farm in Gettysburg and playing golf. Mamie was delighted that John's family had moved into an old schoolhouse situated on their farm. The grandchildren would be close by. There would be challenges ahead, but after moving twenty-eight times in their life together, they would never have to move again.

Chapter 17

The Greatest Honor

The temperature was below freezing as Ike and Mamie climbed into the back seat of their 1955 Chrysler Imperial. John turned to smile at them, then put the car into gear. Slowly they drove through the icy streets of Washington, DC, and out onto the highway. No one spoke. For the first time in years there was no motorcade, no revving police motorbikes, no crowds, just the peaceful quiet of a city cloaked in snow. It was late afternoon when they reached Gettysburg. Small groups of people stood waiting to welcome the first family home for good. Ike smiled at them and waved.

Everyone needed a rest after the election and the hectic two months that had followed. After unpacking their things at the farmhouse, Ike and Mamie headed to Palm Desert, California, for a month's vacation. The place had a wonderful golf course, which Ike intended to make full use of. While in California he began planning his next book, which would cover his White House years in two volumes. He already had a publishing contract and had received a large advance for it.

Having been president, Ike was entitled to continue being called Mr. President for the rest of his life. But he had other plans. Being president was an honor, but the greatest honor in Ike's life was being a US Army general. It would take an act of Congress to restore his military title, but Ike asked President Kennedy to put forward a bill that would do just that. On March 23, 1961, Ike learned the bill had passed Congress. He could now return to being called General Eisenhower. Nothing pleased him more. Before anything else, Ike was a soldier at heart.

On May Day 1962, Ike and Mamie were in Abilene to celebrate the hundredth anniversary of his mother Ida's birth and the opening of the Dwight D. Eisenhower Presidential Library, a large, white-columned building that stood opposite the family home. Twenty-five thousand people, including old neighbors, school friends, dignitaries, and Vice President Lyndon Johnson listened intently as Ike honored his mother in his speech. "I think that all of her sons—indeed, all of her close relatives—would, today, like to think that she knows that they still revere her teachings, her strength, her refusal ever to admit defeat in small or great things. She was truly a remarkable person!" Then Ike reminded the audience that they each had a role to play in preserving democracy in the United States. "America is the strongest nation in the world, and she will never be defeated or damaged seriously by anyone from the outside. Only Americans can ever hurt America."

In August 1963, Ike traveled to Europe to film a documentary with Walter Cronkite of CBS News to commemorate the twentieth anniversary of D-Day the following year. For a month Ike relived the war, returning to his old headquarters at Southwick House. It was eerie to walk inside again. The building had been left exactly as it was when Ike commanded the D-Day invasion from there. A copy of the weather forecast still lay on the table. Ike and Walter Cronkite, who had covered World War II as a reporter, took turns driving the beaches of Normandy, reliving how it was in 1944. On the last day of filming, Ike sat looking at the American Cemetery on the cliffs overlooking Omaha Beach. He was aware that thousands of young men were buried there—young men who had mothers and fathers and wives and sweethearts and children who would be watching the documentary. He spent hours searching for the right words to convey both the tragedy and the heroic nature of these men's sacrifice. With tears in his eyes, Ike looked into the camera and said,

> These young boys, so many of them were cut off in their prime. They had families that grieved for them, but they never knew the great experiences of going through life that my son can enjoy.
>
> I devoutly hope that we will never again

> have to see such scenes . . . these people gave us a chance, and they bought time for us, so that we can do better than we have done before. So every time I come back to these beaches, or any day when I think about that day, twenty years ago now, I say once more we must find some way to work . . . to gain an eternal peace for this world.

Three months later, on Friday, November 22, 1963, Ike was in New York City for a United Nations luncheon when he learned that President Kennedy had been shot in Dallas, Texas. An hour later Ike watched his friend Walter Cronkite on television, his voice cracking with emotion, say, "From Dallas, Texas, the flash, apparently official: 'President Kennedy died at 1 p.m. Central Standard Time.'" Ike hung his head. This was a devastating day for the United States.

As Ike attended President Kennedy's funeral, he began to think about the kind of funeral he wanted.

On November 12, 1965, while vacationing at the Augusta National Golf Course in Georgia, Ike suffered a second heart attack. As he lay in bed recovering, he realized his time left on earth was limited. After surviving two heart attacks he could not expect to survive a third. Ike decided it was time for him to sell his prize-winning Angus cows and rent out his farm. It was also time for him to think more about his own funeral. He and Mamie had agreed they both wanted to be buried beneath the floor of the Place of Meditation at the Eisenhower Library in Abilene.

Ike and Mamie celebrated their fiftieth wedding anniversary on July 1, 1966. They were both acutely aware of how much the times had changed since the long-ago day of their wedding. A musical group called the Beatles was all the rage with their strange rock-and-roll songs. And lots of young people now called themselves hippies. Ike and Mamie struggled to understand how so many things they'd been raised to value were now being rejected by young people.

Following their wedding anniversary, Ike made a secret trip to Denver, where he had Ikky's coffin exhumed and taken by army aircraft to Abilene. With his brother Milton at his side, Ike watched as Ikky's little coffin was lowered into its new resting place under the floor of the Place of Meditation. Even though Ikky had died forty-five years before, a fresh wave of grief overwhelmed Ike as he stood looking down at the stark bronze plaque in the floor that commemorated his first son.

Over the next two years, Ike's health continued to decline. Just before Christmas 1966 he had gall bladder surgery, and in April 1967 he suffered another heart attack. This time he moved permanently into Walter Reed Army Medical Center in Washington, DC. Many people came to visit him, including his old friend Billy Graham, who prayed with him. On his seventy-eighth birthday, Ike sat at his medical center room window, waving heartily as the army band serenaded him outside.

As 1968 drew to a close, not one but two of the Eisenhower grandchildren got married. Anne, who was nineteen years old, married Fernando Echavarría-Uribe in a quiet ceremony. The two had met while Anne was vacationing in Colombia two years before. A month later, David, Ike and Mamie's only grandson, married Julie Nixon, daughter of president-elect Richard Nixon. Ike was too ill to attend either wedding. He knew his remaining time was short.

On March 28, 1969, General Dwight D. Eisenhower died at Walter Reed Army Medical Center. As a former president of the United States and chief of the Allied Forces, Ike was accorded all the pomp and ceremony due him. Bells across the nation tolled while twenty-one-gun salutes cracked through the air. Ike's body lay in state at the Capitol rotunda, and his funeral was held at the Washington National Cathedral. Following the funeral, Ike's casket was loaded onto a train at Union Station in Washington, DC. A huge American flag was draped over the rail-car carrying the casket as it made its way homeward to Abilene, Kansas. Along the way old men in uniform snapped to attention as the train passed, and mothers held up little children to see, hoping they would remember this historic moment for the rest of their lives.

On April 2, 1969, the train arrived in Abilene. After a brief ceremony on the grounds where he had played as a young boy, Ike was laid to rest below the floor of the Place of Meditation. Five-star general Dwight David Eisenhower was buried in his World War II military uniform and, at his insistence, in a government-issued casket.

Bibliography

Ambrose, Stephen E. *Eisenhower: Soldier and President*. New York: Simon & Schuster, 1990.

———. *The Victors: Eisenhower and His Boys: The Men of World War II*. New York: Simon & Schuster, 1998.

Beschloss, Michael R. *Eisenhower: A Centennial Life*. New York: HarperCollins, 1990.

D'Este, Carlo. *Eisenhower: A Soldier's Life*. New York: Henry Holt, 2002.

Eisenhower, David, and Julie Nixon Eisenhower. *Going Home To Glory: A Memoir of Life with Dwight D. Eisenhower 1961–1969*. New York: Simon & Schuster, 2010.

Eisenhower, Dwight D. *Crusade In Europe*. Garden City, NY: Doubleday, 1948.

———. *In Review: Pictures I've Kept: A Concise Pictorial Autobiography*. Garden City, NY: Doubleday, 1969.

———. *Letters To Mamie*. Edited by John S. D. Eisenhower. Garden City, NY: Doubleday, 1978.

Eisenhower, Susan. *Mrs. Ike: Portrait of a Marriage*. Ferrous Books, 2011.

Ferrell, Robert H., ed. *The Eisenhower Diaries*. New York: Norton, 1981.

Humes, James C. *Eisenhower and Churchill: The Partnership That Saved the World.* Roseville, CA: Forum, 2001.

Perret, Geoffrey. *Eisenhower*. Holbrook, MA: Adams Media Corporation, 1999.

Young, Jeff C. *Dwight D. Eisenhower: Soldier and President.* Greensboro, NC: Morgan Reynolds, 2002.

About the Authors

Janet and Geoff Benge are a husband and wife writing team with more than thirty years of writing experience. Janet is a former elementary school teacher. Geoff holds a degree in history. Originally from New Zealand, the Benges spent ten years serving with Youth With A Mission. They have two daughters, Laura and Shannon, and an adopted son, Lito. They make their home in the Orlando, Florida, area.

Also from Janet and Geoff Benge...

More adventure-filled biographies for ages 10 to 100!

Christian Heroes: Then and Now

Gladys Aylward: The Adventure of a Lifetime • 978-1-57658-019-6
Nate Saint: On a Wing and a Prayer • 978-1-57658-017-2
Hudson Taylor: Deep in the Heart of China • 978-1-57658-016-5
Amy Carmichael: Rescuer of Precious Gems • 978-1-57658-018-9
Eric Liddell: Something Greater Than Gold • 978-1-57658-137-7
Corrie ten Boom: Keeper of the Angels' Den • 978-1-57658-136-0
William Carey: Obliged to Go • 978-1-57658-147-6
George Müller: Guardian of Bristol's Orphans • 978-1-57658-145-2
Jim Elliot: One Great Purpose • 978-1-57658-146-9
Mary Slessor: Forward into Calabar • 978-1-57658-148-3
David Livingstone: Africa's Trailblazer • 978-1-57658-153-7
Betty Greene: Wings to Serve • 978-1-57658-152-0
Adoniram Judson: Bound for Burma • 978-1-57658-161-2
Cameron Townsend: Good News in Every Language • 978-1-57658-164-3
Jonathan Goforth: An Open Door in China • 978-1-57658-174-2
Lottie Moon: Giving Her All for China • 978-1-57658-188-9
John Williams: Messenger of Peace • 978-1-57658-256-5
William Booth: Soup, Soap, and Salvation • 978-1-57658-258-9
Rowland Bingham: Into Africa's Interior • 978-1-57658-282-4
Ida Scudder: Healing Bodies, Touching Hearts • 978-1-57658-285-5
Wilfred Grenfell: Fisher of Men • 978-1-57658-292-3
Lillian Trasher: The Greatest Wonder in Egypt • 978-1-57658-305-0
Loren Cunningham: Into All the World • 978-1-57658-199-5
Florence Young: Mission Accomplished • 978-1-57658-313-5
Sundar Singh: Footprints Over the Mountains • 978-1-57658-318-0
C.T. Studd: No Retreat • 978-1-57658-288-6
Rachel Saint: A Star in the Jungle • 978-1-57658-337-1
Brother Andrew: God's Secret Agent • 978-1-57658-355-5
Clarence Jones: Mr. Radio • 978-1-57658-343-2
Count Zinzendorf: Firstfruit • 978-1-57658-262-6
John Wesley: The World His Parish • 978-1-57658-382-1
C. S. Lewis: Master Storyteller • 978-1-57658-385-2
David Bussau: Facing the World Head-on • 978-1-57658-415-6
Jacob DeShazer: Forgive Your Enemies • 978-1-57658-475-0
Isobel Kuhn: On the Roof of the World • 978-1-57658-497-2
Elisabeth Elliot: Joyful Surrender • 978-1-57658-513-9
D. L. Moody: Bringing Souls to Christ • 978-1-57658-552-8
Paul Brand: Helping Hands • 978-1-57658-536-8
Dietrich Bonhoeffer: In the Midst of Wickedness • 978-1-57658-713-3
Francis Asbury: Circuit Rider • 978-1-57658-737-9

Samuel Zwemer: The Burden of Arabia • 978-1-57658-738-6
Klaus-Dieter John: Hope in the Land of the Incas • 978-1-57658-826-2
Mildred Cable: Through the Jade Gate • 978-1-57658-886-4
John Flynn: Into the Never Never • 978-1-57658-898-7
Richard Wurmbrand: Love Your Enemies • 978-1-57658-987-8
Charles Mulli: We Are Family • 978-1-57658-894-9
John Newton: Change of Heart • 978-1-57658-909-0
Helen Roseveare: Mama Luka • 978-1-57658-910-6
Norman Grubb: Mission Builder • 978-1-57658-915-1
Albert Schweitzer • 978-1-57658-961-8

Heroes of History

George Washington Carver: From Slave to Scientist • 978-1-883002-78-7
Abraham Lincoln: A New Birth of Freedom • 978-1-883002-79-4
Meriwether Lewis: Off the Edge of the Map • 978-1-883002-80-0
George Washington: True Patriot • 978-1-883002-81-7
William Penn: Liberty and Justice for All • 978-1-883002-82-4
Harriet Tubman: Freedombound • 978-1-883002-90-9
John Adams: Independence Forever • 978-1-883002-50-3
Clara Barton: Courage under Fire • 978-1-883002-51-0
Daniel Boone: Frontiersman • 978-1-932096-09-5
Theodore Roosevelt: An American Original • 978-1-932096-10-1
Douglas MacArthur: What Greater Honor • 978-1-932096-15-6
Benjamin Franklin: Live Wire • 978-1-932096-14-9
Christopher Columbus: Across the Ocean Sea • 978-1-932096-23-1
Laura Ingalls Wilder: A Storybook Life • 978-1-932096-32-3
Orville Wright: The Flyer • 978-1-932096-34-7
Captain John Smith: A Foothold in the New World • 978-1-932096-36-1
Thomas Edison: Inspiration and Hard Work • 978-1-932096-37-8
Alan Shepard: Higher and Faster • 978-1-932096-41-5
Ronald Reagan: Destiny at His Side • 978-1-932096-65-1
Davy Crockett: Ever Westward • 978-1-932096-67-5
Milton Hershey: More Than Chocolate • 978-1-932096-82-8
Billy Graham: America's Pastor • 978-1-62486-024-9
Ben Carson: A Chance at Life • 978-1-62486-034-8
Louis Zamperini: Redemption • 978-1-62486-049-2
Elizabeth Fry: Angel of Newgate • 978-1-62486-064-5
William Wilberforce: Take Up the Fight • 978-1-62486-057-7
William Bradford: Plymouth's Rock • 978-1-62486-092-8
Ernest Shackleton: Going South • 978-1-62486-093-5
Benjamin Rush: The Common Good • 978-1-62486-123-9

Heroes of History are available in paperback, e-book, and audiobook formats, with more coming soon! Unit Study Curriculum Guides are available for each biography.

www.heroesofhistory.com